THE JESUS BOAT

THE JESUS BOAT

LIVING PROOF OF
A MODERN-DAY MIRACLE IN GALILEE

CHRISTIAN STILLMAN

JESUS BOAT, INC.
www.jesusboatmuseum.com

First Jesus Boat, Inc. hardcover edition January 2009

Jesus Boat is a trademark of Jesus Boat, Inc.

For information about special discounts for bulk purchases, please contact Jesus
Boat, Inc. Special Sales at info@jesusboatmuseum.com

Designed by C. Linda Dingler

Manufactured in the United States of America

10 9 8 7 6 5 4 3 2 1

Library of Congress Cataloging-in-Publication Data
Library of Congress Control Number: 2008938846

ISBN-13: 978-1-4165-8797-2
ISBN-10:   1-4165-8797-7

For Jenny

ACKNOWLEDGEMENTS

It is necessary here to note that the completion of this book would not have been possible were it not for the interest and support of a man named Jack Mahfar. Jack, an Iranian-born Swiss, was a dear friend of General Yigal Allon. His close friendship with the late Allon produced in him a fervent Zionism, which in turn led him to contribute funding to the State of Israel (particularly for public health facilities and research, and the Yigal Allon Museum).

In 1990, ten years after Yigal Allon passed away, Jack visited the boat at the museum, at that point still undergoing preservation treatment. Inspired by the story of the boat, he exclaimed, "So this is the boat of Jesus!" The others with him quickly corrected him, asserting that it was a boat from Jesus' time, but not Jesus' boat. Jack stuck with what he had said before, saying, "I feel that it must be the actual boat on which Jesus sailed with his followers."

This boat has had a profound impact on Jack Mahfar. He has supported the museum financially over the years, and is always looking for ways to help. When I needed to fly to Israel to speak with Kurt Raveh and the Lufan brothers, Jack Mahfar bought the ticket. Jack's continued support has significantly helped the Yigal

Allon Museum with the difficult task of maintaining the boat.

Both Jack and his son Abe have been incredibly helpful over the course of this book being written. I thank them both for their contributions and assistance. I hope that this book will bring many new people to the Yigal Allon Museum, so new generations can see and learn about this miraculous discovery.

As well as Jack Mahfar, I would like to thank everyone else who made this book possible.

First of all, I want to thank Doron and Alon Kossonogi for bringing me onto this project and giving me the opportunity to write my first book and let it be about such an incredible discovery. Gonny, Doron's wife, helped me out considerably with her diligence in immediately translating the interview tapes I brought back with me from Israel. Alon served as an interpreter for me when I needed to communicate with people in Israel—without him, I would have been literally at a loss for words in my interviews. Thanks to Doron and Alon as well for their patience through all of the unforeseen twists and turns that developed over the course of this book, and for putting me in touch with everyone I needed to consult to finish the manuscript.

There is a whole host of people in Israel without whose help I would have been unable to complete this project. Needless to say, without the Lufan brothers, this book wouldn't be here at all. Aside from their initial discovery, however, they volunteered their time to speak with me about the boat, despite my being completely unable to speak Hebrew. Their testimonies from the excavation were invaluable—without them, the story of this boat rings hollow.

Kurt Raveh, as well, was more than willing to help out by filling in gaps in the information I had and spending the better part of a day going over the story of the excavation. His willingness to take time out of his insanely busy schedule ensured that I had the material I needed to piece together the events and understand quite a bit of the story from "behind the scenes."

ACKNOWLEDGEMENTS

I must thank Orna Cohen for her assistance as well. Even though a few in-person meetings in Jerusalem fell through, she offered to do a phone interview and provided me with an understanding of the scientific side of the boat, as well as her own personal testimony from the process. I also must thank Shelley Wachsmann, who graciously gave me permission to scavenge his book for any and all information I could glean from it—his story first taught me about the boat, and his comprehensive, academic coverage of the excavation provided the backbone of my own initial knowledge of the Jesus boat.

Though she didn't play a role in the excavation of the boat, Marina Banai of the Yigal Allon Museum was a priceless person to know. She helped me get news articles, images, and information about the Sea of Galilee, and was always willing to do more—I'd be afraid to see the state of this book if I hadn't had help from Marina. Additionally, Nir Rottenberg, the current manager of the Yigal Allon Museum, has been a great help and has supported the writing of this book in every possible way.

Thanks to my father for bringing me into this project in the first place. When I traveled to Israel for the first time, it was at his insistence that I see this boat. Six months later he asked if I would like to write a book about it as I finished college. He was a huge asset for me, helping out with deadlines and figuring out exactly what we needed to keep the project moving. I thank both him and my mother, who reviewed and edited the rough copies of my chapters. I couldn't have done it without their help and support.

Finally, I would like to thank my wife, Jenny. She put up with me while I was writing this book, during which time I graduated from college and we planned our wedding. Her love and support helped to keep me going whenever I got stuck, and I am extremely grateful for her understanding each time a new delay popped up.

CHRISTIAN STILLMAN

CONTENTS

THE JESUS BOAT

THE THING THAT SHOULD NOT BE

The base of Jesus' early ministry, the Sea of Galilee—or Lake Kinneret, as it is known in Israel—is one of the most important locations for the Christian faith. Many of the stories in the New Testament take place around the Sea of Galilee, and it was from this region that Jesus called his disciples to follow him. Its biblical context is not the only reason for this small inland lake's celebrity—at around 212 meters, or nearly 700 feet below sea level, the Sea of Galilee is the lowest freshwater lake in the world.

This lake supports Israel's life and agriculture today, and it served the same purpose in the past. The region around the Sea of Galilee thrived because of the fishing industry, and Jesus' first disciples were fishermen themselves. Early in the Gospels, Jesus is located near the Sea of Galilee, and some of the Gospels even have Jesus back at the lake after the Resurrection. When many Christians think of Jesus' ministry, images of the shores of the Galilee pop effortlessly to mind. Clearly, God and the authors of these books believed the Sea of Galilee to be important, and subsequently it exists as one of the central focuses in the climax of the entire biblical story.

Even to non-Christians, the Sea of Galilee is important. Only a few decades after Christ's ministry, the lake was the site of a naval battle between the Jews and the Romans during the period of Roman occupation. The Romans, with greater training, manpower, and resources, overpowered the ill-equipped rebels, filling the Sea of Galilee with the bodies of the slain. The Roman forces killed every last Jewish fighter, and just as the rebels' dead littered the lake, so many of their boats were abandoned and left neglected in the water.

Considering everything that had happened around this inland lake, from historical and religious standpoints and all of the merchant and transport traffic that must have been upon it, it is astounding that no ancient boats had ever been found. The Sea of Galilee, in the time of the New Testament, had fourteen[1] thriving ports and must have had hundreds of boats on it, yet not one of these had survived to modern times.

When one thinks about how many great ships have been raised from ocean depths—or if unable to be raised, were at least discovered relatively intact—it is unfathomable that no boats had ever been found in this small, heavily traveled inland lake.

The reason for the absence of any watercraft surviving in the Sea of Galilee is that warm oxygen-rich freshwater breeds wood borers, bacteria that destroy organic materials such as the wood with which ancient ships were built. Any wooden boats abandoned in the Sea of Galilee in ancient times would literally have been eaten away over the passing years. However, these same bacteria that destroy wooden vessels in the Sea of Galilee are unable to survive in the harsh conditions found in bodies of saltwater or deep freshwater. This is why the Mediterranean Sea and the depths of the Black Sea have yielded up such treasures as the Kyrenia shipwreck off the coast of Cyprus and Robert Ballard's recent Black Sea discoveries.

Archaeologists had searched the Sea of Galilee in underwater dives but had never found any ships. Pottery, anchors, and other artifacts had turned up, and there had been numerous accounts of watercraft on the lake throughout history, but because of the bacterial conditions, people had given up hope that any ancient wooden boats would ever be discovered. It would be foolish to believe that an ancient wooden boat could be found after sitting in the water for hundreds or even thousands of years.

After all, wooden boats, during their lifetime of usage, will start to show wear and must be treated and repaired in order to remain functional. After being used for decades, much of the wood would likely start falling apart. Once a boat is deemed beyond repair, or simply not worth repairing further, it is usually salvaged for any reusable wood left, discarding the remainder. At this point the planking and frames would be in fairly sore condition already. Once such a wreck has been discarded, it shouldn't take long for wood-eating bacteria to fully destroy whatever scavenging boatwrights have left.

This book, and others on the same topic, ought never to have been written. What is described in the following pages ought never to have happened. It goes against reason and logic. When told that an ancient wooden boat could be found in the Sea of Galilee prior to 1986, nautical archaeologists would have dismissed such an idea. They would have declared it impossible for a wooden boat to survive in such conditions. Barring a miracle, they would have been right.

But this is a book about the amazing discovery of a wooden boat that did survive, despite contrary logic and evidence. For almost 2,000 years in the freshwater of the Sea of Galilee, this boat lasted against all odds. Like the re-establishment of Israel and much of what is recorded in the Old and New Testaments, it doesn't necessarily make sense and it goes against reason, but nonetheless the proof is undeniable.

The one thing that is most important in this whole story is the fact that this boat connects modern Christians with their Lord and Savior in a completely new way. This discovery repaints the sections of the Gospels that take place around the Sea of Galilee in a light previously unseen. Despite paintings of Jesus walking on water and calming the storm, no one knew what the disciples' boat would have looked like. Now, for the first time, we do.

The boat isn't an idol, nor should it be seen as an object of worship. However, it ought to be seen as an incredible devotional tool. This boat breathes fresh life into the old, familiar Bible stories, allowing Christians to understand, as the disciples did, the significance of Jesus' actions. It can make us feel more like we are walking with our Lord.

Some have dubbed this boat the "Miracle Boat." It certainly deserves that title, for throughout the events of excavation and conservation, it seemed that God was guiding and protecting the whole process. So many things about this boat are nothing short of extraordinary and as this book will show, this boat is as much of a modern-day miracle as there ever has been.

1

A Fisherman's Tale

The Sea of Galilee, located in northern Israel, serves its country year after year as a natural reservoir. In Israel's hot, dry climate, it is imperative that fresh water be available both for consumption by its citizens and for the country's agricultural needs, and the Sea of Galilee provides that life-giving water. In 1986, Israel was struggling in the midst of a serious drought, the result of inadequate rainfall over the immediately preceding years.

To lessen the difficulties of such situations, Israel pumps water out of the Sea of Galilee in order to bring it to those parts of the country that are without their own water source. This was the case with the drought that carried over into 1986. Pumping water out of the Sea of Galilee, however, is not an ideal solution for everyone. Those who live on its shores, particularly fishermen, have the unpleasant experience of seeing their lake and livelihoods slowly dry up.

Imagine the mindset of the people living by the Sea of Galilee during such a drought. While the rest of the country is receiving water, these people cannot help but see what such provision is costing. Daily, as the pumps bring water to the country's parched regions, these people can see just how finite the water source is. The river water and occasional light rainfall that try to replenish the lake are proving inadequate, and they see the lake get lower every day.

As the water level recedes daily, cities and towns on the shore of the lake are left high and dry. Droughts like this can push the water line back hundreds of feet, stranding docks in mud and weeds. Galilean cities such as Tiberias and Capernaum were constructed initially for fishing and maritime trade and travel. With the decreased

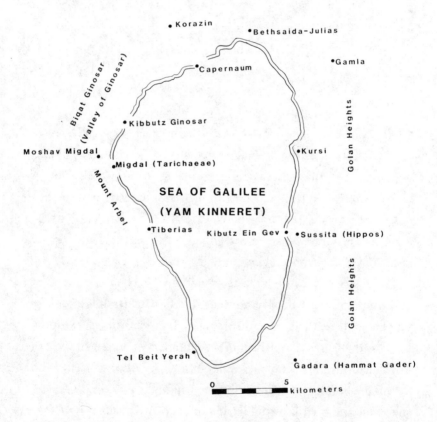

The Sea of Galilee

water level, those who live in the cities and settlements around the lake find their lives immensely more difficult.

On the northwestern shore of the Sea of Galilee, about 7 kilometers down the coast from Capernaum, lies Kibbutz Ginosar. Ginosar, like other Israeli kibbutzim, is a cooperative settlement in which property is owned communally. Kibbutzim were created in the Zionist movement as Jews began to move back to Israel from Europe in the early decades of the twentieth century. These settlements continued to be built, even after the end of the British Mandate Period and the start of Israeli independence.

The kibbutzim around Israel are actually one of the main reasons a modern Jewish state exists today. David Ben-Gurion and General Yigal Allon, prominent figures in the beginning of Israel's modern statehood, were both active kibbutz members. They and their fellow kibbutzniks provided the military backbone during the 1948 Arab-Israeli War. Because of their courage and sacrifice, they won their country's freedom for the first time since the annexation of ancient Israel as a Roman province in 63 B.C.

These communal societies have provided modern Israel with many of its political leaders, and over the years a significant portion of the Israeli army has come from the country's kibbutzim. The importance of the kibbutzim to Israel must not be underestimated. Without the kibbutzim, there would be no modern Israel.

Without Kibbutz Ginosar, this boat would never have been found.

Ginosar is the modern-day incarnation of the biblical city of Gennesaret, and it sits directly on the shores of the Galilee between Capernaum and Migdal (biblical Magdala). The Sea of Galilee overflows with history and significance for hundreds of millions of people around the globe, and holds great importance for Christianity as the cradle of Jesus' ministry.

Two brothers, kibbutzniks from Ginosar, were raised and spent their lives by the shores of the Sea of Galilee. For generations, their ancestors had been fishermen and Moshe (Moishele) and Yuval (Yuvi) Lufan continued the family tradition. Yuvi, for one, is so deeply connected to the sea that there is no smell on earth he prefers to fresh fish and the mud of the Sea of Galilee. Despite their heritage and unlike their neighbors, the Lufan brothers relished the dropping water level of the Sea of Galilee.

From an early age, each of the brothers loved to spend time walking up and down the coastline, eagerly scanning the ground beneath his feet for signs of lost artifacts from long ago. Both Yuvi and Moishele had felt from their childhood that the Sea of Galilee would one day give them an amazing gift. Their frequent beachcombing was a result of that feeling.

Yuvi has become an artist in the kibbutz, but even as a child he loved to draw. His early artwork didn't have a lot of diversity, though. By the age of four, he only drew one thing: boats. His family knew ahead of time what would be on the paper when he drew something, and each sketch he showed them elicited a groan: "Not a boat again!" Raised in a fishing community, it isn't surprising that boats would play such an important part in his youthful artistic endeavors, but to look back now it appears an incredible coincidence that Yuvi should have been so obsessed with them.

For years the brothers had longed to find some great treasure hidden in the Sea of Galilee, but it seemed too much to ask that the treasure they'd find be a boat. The Sea of Galilee had been searched countless times and no boat had ever been found. The archaeological community had, by this point, given up hope that such a find was possible, though the brothers from Ginosar were thankfully not aware that the odds of finding their hoped-for boat were just about zero.

As frequently as they were able, Yuvi and Moishele were out

searching the shores of the Sea of Galilee for whatever they could find. It isn't terribly difficult to find something ancient along the water's edge if you know what you're looking for. Yuvi and Moishele had found plenty of small artifacts, like the rocks with holes bored through them used for seine net or dragnet anchors. These easy-to-find relics weren't quite what they were looking for, though, and they inspected as much of the muddy shoreline as they could in their hunts.

That's why the drought was such a blessing for the brothers. Unable to search for artifacts in the water, they could only search on dry land. The prolonged drought and the newly created shoreline provided them with an opportunity they could never have had on their own.

On a clear, chilly day in January 1986, the Lufan brothers went out for a familiar walk along the shore of the Sea of Galilee, headed southwest toward Migdal. There had just been a sharkia, a wind so strong it had cleaned the beaches of weeds and shrubbery. With the beaches clear, now was a perfect time to go "artifact hunting." They were going to a particular stretch of beach they hoped would yield something special.

Months earlier, a military truck had gotten stuck in the mud there. The truck's driver knew he had to get his vehicle out, but it wouldn't prove to be easy. Struggling to free the truck, he spun the wheels in a desperate attempt to find traction. The tires finally found a surface to grip and the truck was able to drive off the beach.

Yuvi and Moishele knew about the truck's escape from the mud, and decided that the beach where it had gotten trapped would be a good place to survey. They walked along the shore until they came to the place where the truck had been stuck. It was easy to find: The site lay in the shadow of three slender palm trees.

"One day," Moishele recounts, "I was walking there and spotted a few coins on the sand the truck had raised. We found many coins in the past, and I cannot explain why I felt there was something special there of a kind we had never found before."

They continued to look around the site, and it paid off. The spinning tires had dug deep into the soft earth, and the mud they sprayed up had contained the ancient coins Moishele found. After he called his brother over, the brothers found more coins. Was it possible these coins were part of a greater treasure hiding just below the surface?

"I have a feeling there is something more in here," Moishele told his brother. "I don't know why, but I have a sense that we can find bigger things in here." Since this area had yielded treasure before, it wasn't too much for him to think that it may do so again.

Years later, Moishele still says, "I can't explain why and how we felt that there was something special there, since we saw not even one piece of wood and we didn't touch or dig to check."

Remember that Moishele, as well as his brother, was born and raised in a kibbutz. Created in the Zionist movement, kibbutzim are completely secular establishments. Not a man of faith, therefore, Moishele is hesitant to ascribe anything to the miraculous. Even so, he admits today that other than God's guidance, there is no explanation for why he felt so drawn to that particular location.

The brothers continued to return to the same site over the next week to see what else they could find. Moishele was absolutely convinced that something more lay buried just beneath the mud, and Yuvi felt sure that the Sea of Galilee was finally going to give them a present.

———

Yuvi told me a story about a poor fisherman's daughter, a girl about six years old. Her father took her into town for a treat one day, and while they walked about something in a store caught the girl's eye.

Sitting there on display was a big doll, and the young girl immediately wanted to have it. Her father told her, sadly, that because they were so poor, he could not buy it for her. They had to return home without the doll.

Once home, the girl did not forget about the doll, and every day went out to sing by the sea that she might be able to have a doll like the one she saw in town that day. For three years she did this, and then one day a strong wind came up on the sea. After the wind had subsided, she walked out, looking along the beach, and saw something like a small boat floating in the water.

After an hour or so, the girl could tell that it was not a boat at all, but was in fact a chest floating toward the beach. She waited until it washed ashore and then went to look at it. Opening the chest, she discovered that inside it was a doll, the same doll she had seen in town three years before.

Yuvi tells this story because he believes that, like the fisherman's daughter, the Sea of Galilee had a gift for Moishele and him. Because they were patient, she (the Galilee) rewarded them just as the little girl had been rewarded.

———

Yuvi tends to walk quickly while looking for pieces of ancient pottery or antique Roman glass on the surface of the mud, and was doing so that day. Moishele scanned the ground a bit more thoroughly than his older brother, and because of that it isn't surprising that a week after he found the coins, Moishele called his older brother over to look at something.

He had found an ancient iron nail.

Not just one nail, either. Spaced a few inches apart in what appeared to be an intentional pattern, nails dotted the beach, hinting at an outline beneath the mud.

The brothers quickly began to dig in the mud to see what was

Yuvi stands over the boat

buried just out of sight. They cleaned up around the nails, and before long, they exposed a piece of wood and knew that they had found something special. Rather than continuing to dig down to uncover it, they dug around it and revealed the outline of a boat in the surface of the mud.

Yuvi and Moishele had spent their whole lives looking on the shores of the Sea of Galilee to find some treasure, a treasure they sincerely believed would eventually turn up. After a lifetime of hunting through the muddy banks, picking up broken pieces of pottery and ancient anchor-stones, the brothers had finally found something truly amazing. Not only had they finally discovered a treasure they had dreamed about for years, but it was one that no one else believed was even possible!

The brothers were overwhelmed with enthusiasm, and understandably so. Their lifelong dream had come true! Yuvi says today that throughout the entire period of excavation, he was so happy he felt as though he was flying. He describes his euphoria as that for months, his feet didn't touch the ground.

Even though they had been longing for this discovery all their lives, they tried hard to stay grounded and realized they had to keep the boat quiet to keep it safe. In order to do this, and to make sure that their enthusiasm was warranted, Moishele and Yuvi agreed to bring their father out to look at the boat.

Their father, Yantshe, was in charge of all of the fishermen in Kibbutz Ginosar at the time, and was well acquainted with boats. If there had been a boat sunk at that site in relatively recent years, their father would know about it. They knew that they needed to run their discovery by him to see what he thought, and so they kept the boat covered that no one else might find it.

When Yantshe's sons brought him out to the site of the boat, he immediately commented that, if the boat was buried as it was in the mud, it was not from his time. Because it was so well buried, he was certain it had to be ancient. He told his sons that he didn't know how old the boat was, but that it was very, very old.

Yuvi and Moishele knew that their father's pronouncement on the boat's antiquity was trustworthy. While they did not know the exact age of the boat, they were now confident that their discovery was an ancient treasure.

Because such a find needed to be properly taken care of and preserved, the brothers and their father decided they ought to talk with a woman named Nitza, at that time the manager of the Yigal Allon Museum (the museum at Ginosar commemorating the Zionist general and co-founder of modern-day Israel).

Three weeks prior to the brothers finding the boat, Moishele had gone to talk with Nitza about the museum. At the time, the museum was still being constructed, but it was almost complete. Because it was a new, big museum he felt that there ought to be some artifacts from the Sea of Galilee on display there.

Without hesitation, Nitza had rejected the idea. "No way," was the phrase she used, according to Moishele. She was adamant that the museum be all about the period from the Palmach—the Israeli military fighting force established toward the end of the British Mandate—to the present.

Moishele argued with her, stressing that there were many interesting things around the Sea of Galilee, but still Nitza would not budge. The plan for the museum was firmly established, and there would be no artifacts.

Once Yuvi and Moishele had found the boat, they returned to the museum and Nitza to petition her once again. Even if some of the typical artifacts from the Sea of Galilee would not be displayed in the museum, surely something as incredible as an ancient fishing boat would be.

Nitza did not believe that the boat belonged in a museum like the Yigal Allon Museum, which was devoted to social, rather than archeological, history, and told the brothers the boat would not be displayed there. She did, however, agree that something needed to be done for the boat and put Moishele and Yuvi in touch with a man named Mendel Nun, a kibbutznik from Ein Gev (across the Sea of Galilee) considered one of the foremost authorities on the Sea of Galilee.

Mendel Nun is deeply connected with the Sea of Galilee. Walking along the shores of the lake, Yuvi explained to me that Nun had been the first to identify the small stones with holes drilled through their centers as weights for fishing nets. Because of that contribution, the miniature seine-net anchors are referred to as "Mendel stones." If anyone would know what to do with an ancient boat, it would surely be Mendel Nun.

He came the next day, but much to the brothers' disappointment he refused to make any claims about the boat. Nun was honest and told the brothers that although he knew a lot about ancient ports, he didn't know much regarding ancient wood. Knowing that he did not possess the knowledge necessary to make an accurate pronouncement, Nun instead brought in a renowned archaeologist from Haifa University, Avner Raban, to verify the boat's antiquity.

When Raban arrived at the boat's location, the two brothers couldn't wait for him see their discovery. After all, since their father could tell the boat was ancient, they only needed the archaeologist to tell them just how old it was.

He was anxious to look at the boat, as well. Never had an ancient boat been found in the Sea of Galilee, or in any similar freshwater conditions for that matter. If this discovery were true, it would be a first and he was eager to be a part of it. The brothers uncovered a section of the boat for Raban to see, and breathlessly waited to hear what he had to say.

It certainly wasn't what they were expecting. He stood up, wiped his hands of mud, and told Yuvi and Moishele that the boat, their precious gift from the Sea of Galilee, was in fact not ancient. It wasn't even old, at least considering the history of the place it was found. He told the two kibbutznik brothers that their boat was at best 300 years old.

If the brothers had been emotionally flying before, they now came crashing into the muddy beach.

Finding something a few hundred years old in the United States would be pretty exciting—a turn-of-the-century artifact, maybe something left over from either the Civil or Revolutionary Wars. As a modern nation, the United States doesn't even have 300 years of history, unless one counts the colonial period. However, in Israel, or elsewhere in the Middle East for that matter, 300 years is a drop in the historical bucket. When the archaeologist told Yuvi and

Moishele that the boat they had found was 300 years old or newer, what he said basically meant that their find had the same significance as digging up a lost pair of sunglasses on the beach.

Fortunately for everyone, the brothers refused to believe Raban's assessment of the boat. They trusted their father's initial assessment and paid no attention to what the archaeologist had had to say about their discovery. Adamant that they were correct, Yuvi and Moishele persuaded Nun to connect them with the Department of Antiquities.

There were two nautical archaeologists working for the Israeli Department of Antiquities at the time they were called to take a look at the boat, Kurt Raveh and Shelley Wachsmann. Because no one believed a boat such as this could be found in the Sea of Galilee, and because the conditions presented to ancient wood by salt water are much more favorable, Kurt and Shelley were working on Israel's Mediterranean coast at an ancient site called Dor.

Dor used to be a thriving port, serving as one of the main entryways into the country from the Mediterranean Sea. It had a natural harbor, but because of how the breaker islands are formed, it was a fairly difficult task to safely bring a ship in to dock. Since the navigational conditions were so treacherous, there are many wrecks around Dor. In addition to the shipwrecks, Napoleon, returning from his Egyptian campaign, was forced to throw most of his weaponry into the sea at Dor in order to have adequate transport to bring his wounded soldiers back home.

Just prior to the call that told Kurt and Shelley about the boat in the Sea of Galilee, a large storm had been raging in the Mediterranean at Dor. This storm presented the two archaeologists with an incredible opportunity—the turmoil in the sea and the tossing waves had uncovered a lot of artifacts that they would otherwise have been unable to reach.

Having such a bounty of treasure just at their fingertips, in the sea at their "home base"—an old glass factory that had been converted into a museum—was not a prospect either Kurt or Shelley was willing to pass up. They decided to search the Dor seabed before driving across Israel to Ginosar. They knew they would find ancient treasures sunk beneath the waves of the Mediterranean, and it would be a waste of time and opportunity if they rushed to Galilee on a wild goose chase. After all, they both knew that no boat had ever been found in the Sea of Galilee despite extensive prior searches, and both were extremely skeptical that what had been found truly was what the report claimed it to be.

When Shelley and Kurt finally packed up their gear to drive inland to Ginosar, they didn't know what kind of expedition they were in for. Since they'd only been informed that a boat, presumably ancient, had been found in the Sea of Galilee, their Jeep was loaded with dive gear. Both men assumed that the message was literally true: The boat was still beneath the waters of the Sea of Galilee.

A dive into the Sea of Galilee was not a pleasant scenario for Shelley. He had been on dives into her waters before, and was not fond of the conditions of the freshwater lake. In his book The Sea of Galilee Boat: An Extraordinary 2000-Year-Old Discovery, Shelley Wachsmann briefly relates stories of diving in the Sea of Galilee. In these recollections, Shelley notes the water's murkiness and how the silt clouds up so that a few inches in front of your eyes, you cannot even see your hand.[1]

Kurt also had experience diving in the Sea of Galilee, and he says that the visibility was so bad, dive partners had to be connected with rope or they would get completely separated from each other. Searching for a boat in conditions such as these was not appealing, especially since both archaeologists doubted the genuineness of the message they had received.

Despite the dive conditions that awaited them, both Kurt and Shelley were willing to investigate the discovery. On the off chance that the boat found by the Lufan brothers truly was ancient, it would be the discovery of a lifetime.

A few days had transpired from the time Yuvi and Moishele had initially discovered the boat to when Kurt and Shelley drove northeast to reach the Sea of Galilee. Both men still recall passing the sign on the road indicating the point at which the road started to drop below sea level. Both also remember joking that if there truly were an ancient boat where they were headed, it would be the lowest wreck excavation in the world. Neither of the archaeologists even imagined that the boat would have been found on dry land.

When they first got to Ginosar, they met with Yuvi and Moishele in the kibbutz's hotel over coffee. The brothers began explaining the site and what they had found to Kurt and Shelley, and told them that they had found iron nails around the boat.

When the archaeologists heard that there were iron nails in the boat, they were disheartened. They felt as though they had been brought out for nothing; if there were iron nails, it signified the boat was probably from the Arabic or Turkish period, not nearly as old as they had been hoping for.

Shelley and Kurt then asked the brothers if the boat had mortise and tenon joints. Neither Yuvi nor Moishele even knew what the archaeologists meant by mortise and tenon joints, so Kurt and Shelley drew out a diagram for them on a napkin. Mortise and tenon is the name for a joint in which two planks are attached by cutting holes in the edges and fitting a flat peg between them. Once the peg joins the two planks together, additional pegs are drilled through the planks, fixing everything in place.

Showing them what the joint looked like, Kurt told the two kibbutzniks that the next time they find what seems to be an ancient boat, to check for this kind of pegged joint before they call him and Shelley back. After all, it seemed such a waste of time to spend a day coming out to Galilee when a massive storm had just subsided at Dor and there was plenty of work to be done there.

Since they had taken the time to come to Ginosar, they decided to go and have a look at the boat anyway, though the archaeologists were convinced that the boat was not ancient after all. Joined by Nitza and Mendel Nun, they left the hotel and their coffee and headed out to the beach.

On the way out to the boat, Yuvi and Moishele told Shelley and Kurt that a few days before, another archaeologist had come to take

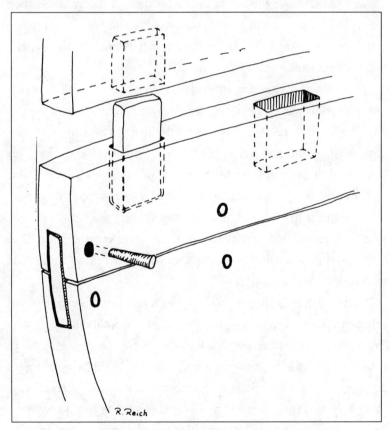

Diagram of mortise and tenon joints in boat construction

a look at it. They told the two men that their colleague didn't think it was ancient and that it was probably from the Turkish period. Upon hearing this, Kurt was even more frustrated that they had come out to Ginosar to see a boat that had already been confirmed as not ancient, but at this point they were already at the site of the boat.

They all started to dig where Yuvi and Moishele said the boat was, and Kurt and Shelley were immediately amazed. As soon as the wood was revealed, they could see exactly the same mortise and tenon joints they had drawn for the brothers on the napkin back at the hotel.

Kurt pointed out the joints to the brothers and confirmed their belief: While they couldn't pinpoint exactly the boat's age, it was certainly not Turkish. It was either ancient Roman or Greek, and the brothers were right.

A current of excitement immediately jumped through everyone. Yuvi and Moishele's confidence had paid off. Kurt and Shelley began jumping around, yelling, "You are on the map!" Two fishermen had done what numerous archaeologists had been unable to do: They had found the only ancient boat ever to survive in the Galilee!

They still needed to confirm the boat's age, however. They went back to the Jeep and grabbed the few shovels they had brought. With a fever of amazement still settling down on the group, they began to dig an outline of the boat in the mud so that they could start to learn more about it.

As they carefully dug around the boat, revealing its shape in the soft earth, an amazing thing happened. Massive, threatening storm clouds began to gather overhead, blocking out the sunlight. All of a sudden the clouds opened up and torrential rain began to pour down, snapping the region's long drought. The rainfall was so heavy that everyone dropped their shovels and ran to the Jeep for cover.

The storm only lasted a few minutes, and as the rain subsided the group looked up in the sky and saw yet another amazing sight.

Above their heads, a magnificent double rainbow arced across the Sea of Galilee. At this, everyone broke out screaming and shouting, looking up at the rainbow and dancing around. Although no one present at the time was a person of faith, the rainbow was taken as a sign, as with the rainbow God showed Noah after the flood. They felt as though they had received a blessing to excavate the boat.

Not everyone felt the same way.

2

Digging In

Despite the best efforts of the Lufan brothers and Yantshe, Nitza, Kurt, Shelley, and Mendel Nun, rumors of the boat were about to spread like wildfire throughout the long-parched region. Unfortunately, much of the news that got around so fast was based on rumor rather than factual information. Because of this, most of those who heard about the boat were more interested than they would have been with a typical archaeological find.

In Israel, a land blessed with a rich history and hundreds of thousands of artifacts, important discoveries happen on a fairly regular basis. Each new artifact unearthed by archaeologists certainly wouldn't excite the interest of the general populace. There must have been something more to the story of this boat.

The initial group of rescuers, with the go-ahead they had received from Kurt and Shelley's pronouncement of the boat as ancient, had been in contact with the Israeli Department of Antiquities. Everyone involved knew a great treasure had been found, and it needed to be excavated and preserved. Shelley believed it would be best to let the water level rise up again and cover the boat, so that the excavation would be underwater.

When they had uncovered the boat to look at it, it was obvious that the timbers were extremely waterlogged. The hull of the boat looked, at first glance, to be in fairly decent shape, but the wood had a soggy, spongy, and crumbly texture to it. If one were to touch the wood, it would feel like wet cardboard, barely holding together. During the nearly 2,000 years the boat had sat under the mud, most of the wood cells in the frames and planking had been replaced by water.

Shelley and Kurt understood that the prolonged exposure of the boat to air would cause the wood to dry out, and the beating sun during the day in Israel, even in late winter, would ensure that the boat would dry out fast. If the wood of the boat dried out, it would be unable to support its own weight and would crumble to pieces. The best solution they could think of to keep this scenario from happening was to have an underwater excavation, even though visibility would be poor.

If the excavation were to wait until the water level rose sufficiently, there was no telling how long it would take. With the sudden rainstorm that brought the double rainbow, the drought seemed to have been broken, but the water level of the Sea of Galilee was not under Kurt and Shelley's control. A preliminary, investigatory dig would need to take place soon, but the real excavation would have to be postponed until the water came up well over the boat.

Such a delay was to be expected, anyway. The Department of Antiquities, an overstretched and insufficiently funded government bureaucracy, could not be expected to make any sort of timely decision to excavate. It would take months, the department said, for the funding to be allocated and for staff and resources to be gathered. After a rush of excitement, it seemed like the only option open to the kibbutzniks and archaeologists was to wait.

This was devastating news for Yuvi and Moishele. They believed that the boat had been presented to them at this specific time and this was their only opportunity to rescue it. The boat had revealed itself to the world, and if they didn't take care of it immediately, they would lose it. They were crushed, but the decision was out of their hands. They had no choice but to wait.

And they would have waited, if the story had not been leaked to the media.

Once the archaeological community began buzzing with the news that a verifiably ancient boat had been discovered in the Sea of Galilee, Avner Raban, the archaeologist who had arrived first on the scene and pronounced the boat a modern-age ship, learned of his mistake. He may have been embarrassed and probably did not want word to spread of his inaccurate assessment, so he rushed to the Israeli newspapers. He told them that an ancient boat had been found in the Sea of Galilee, the first and only such one ever to survive. On top of that, Raban let them know that he was the one responsible for its discovery.

While that was not true, he was at least partly responsible for its rescue. Raban's disclosure to the media resulted in a rapidly spreading interest in the boat, and that media coverage and public interest played an important part in its rescue.

Shelley and Kurt still needed to execute the initial investigation of the boat before they could make any final, official recommendations to the Department of Antiquities. Before they could do that, the group had to get licenses from that same department in order to legally work on the boat. It took about a week for the licenses to come through, and once the documentation came, they were able to begin the trial excavation.

The cooking pot found near the boat

During the preliminary excavation, the crew dug in the mud in and alongside the boat to get a closer look at its wood. While digging outside the boat, Nitza made the first supplementary discovery at the site: She found an oil lamp—a miniature, clay version of Aladdin's lamp—which from its style could be dated to the first century A.D.

"This really blew our minds," Kurt said. "When we found the lamp, we knew it was first century. We were in business."

In addition to the oil lamp, a cooking pot and some additional potsherds were found, but all outside of the boat. The boat had not been carrying a cargo when the mud had buried it. Because of the proximity of the pottery the excavators could give a rough estimate of when the ship was in use, but accurate confirmation of the boat's age would have to wait until some of the timbers could be tested using the carbon-14 dating method.

During this preliminary excavation, there had been a film crew from the Israeli Television Authority on site to record footage of the dig. It had been agreed that they would not release any of their footage until the boat was announced to the press, but the plan was to keep the boat quiet until the water level had risen again and covered the boat.

The story that Raban leaked broke shortly after the probe dig.

Following the preliminary excavation of the boat, Shelley was in Jerusalem to discuss the team's recommendations with officials from the Department of Antiquities. While at their offices, he was shown a page from that day's newspaper, in which a small story on the boat was printed on an inside page. That article was likely the result of Raban's disclosure to the media that an ancient boat had been found at Ginosar.

Everyone hoped desperately that the story would go unnoticed, and that the short article would be the extent of the media coverage for a while. The tiny article, however, opened the floodgates.

Since the press had already aired the story, there was nothing keeping the Israeli Television Authority from capitalizing on the exclusive footage that they had from the probe dig in their sole possession. Almost immediately, the local media coverage exploded uncontrollably.

Two main stories circulated about the boat. One was fairly factual. It told of the boat being found and explained that it had been dated to the time of Jesus' ministry (which had not yet been confirmed, at least not conclusively). The other story was much more of a rumor, and because of that was much more dangerous for the boat.

That story went something like this:

In World War I, the Ottomans and the British were fighting in Palestine. The Sea of Galilee being a key waterway, the Turkish army utilized ships to transport gold for commissions and pay for its officers and soldiers toward the south. Taking advantage of this,

British planes flew overhead and bombed one such boat laden with gold. It sank in the lake, and its cargo was never recovered.

When people began hearing that a boat had been found in the Sea of Galilee, many immediately thought that it could be the same Turkish boat that the British sunk during WWI. The dream of finding a shipwreck filled with gold coins was too much temptation to resist. After all, had it not been coins on the surface of the mud that had drawn Moishele and Yuvi to the boat?

Even if it were not the Turkish boat, surely the "Jesus Boat," as some were starting to call it, would be worth quite a bit of money. Any number of people would be interested in buying Jesus' fishing boat, so regardless of what cargo it may or may not have contained, the scramble was on to find and dig the boat up.

Thankfully, the brothers and the archaeologists had anticipated the inevitable public interest in the boat and had taken measures to protect it. Since they had not known when the boat would be approved for excavation, as well as to protect it from the elements, the group had carefully re-buried the boat under the mud.

To protect it from treasure seekers, they took care to make the site look as natural as if the water had just receded from that stretch of beach. Yuvi and Moishele then borrowed a tractor from the kibbutz and strewed debris about the site, hoping this would disguise the site of the boat's location and protect the boat from tractors and trucks driving over it.

Taking extra caution, the two brothers went further down the beach and dug two fake excavation sites, hoping to throw people off the trail of the real one. They had waited all their lives for this discovery, and they were going to do everything in their power to make sure it wasn't taken away.

Despite all of the measures Yuvi, Moishele, and the others had taken to protect the boat from treasure hunters, they all knew they could not wait indefinitely for the excavation to get underway. If they did, they were only too aware that they didn't have the manpower and resources to keep the boat permanently guarded. Everybody knew it was only a matter of time before some treasure hunter actually found the boat.

———

Kurt Raveh, one of the lead archaeologists on the dig, told me a story about a colleague of his, Claire Epstein. Claire worked as an archaeologist for the Department of Antiquities, and had also been a member of Kibbutz Ginosar. One time, she had been working on an excavation in the Golan Heights and went to check on the site at night. Upon her arrival at the excavation site, she saw a group of men with lights and shovels, trying to dig up any valuable artifacts they could find before the archaeologists returned in the morning.

Determined to protect the site from the plunderers, Claire began yelling at the men in an attempt to scare them away. The robbers had come well prepared, however, and pulled out their guns when they heard Claire. She was forced to run away, but escaped intact. Unfortunately, Kurt couldn't say whether or not the police arrived in time to save everything at the excavation site—by the time the authorities got there, the thieves probably had enough time to find and steal some artifacts and get away.

———

Kurt and Shelley in particular were acutely aware of the growing danger facing the ancient boat. Many dig sites have been plundered before an excavation can be completed, and Kurt told me that over 60% of the artifacts discovered in Israel wind up stolen or on the black market. As the threat of looting increased with the growing media coverage, they knew they had to act, and fast. If not, they risked coming to check on the site some morning and finding a hole where they had left the boat.

Shelley decided to propose an immediate excavation to the Department of Antiquities, but to do so he needed to come up with a plan of how the excavation would run. He called a colleague, a renowned conservator named Orna Cohen with whom they had worked in the past. After discussing the situation, Orna agreed to come and work on the project with Shelley and Kurt. Shelley asked her to come out to Ginosar the following day, and to prepare a report for the Department of Antiquities outlining the anticipated difficulties of the excavation and a rough estimate of what the whole process would cost.

The day after Orna came on board, everyone involved with the boat came to the hotel at Ginosar for a meeting. Avi Eitan, the director of the Department of Antiquities, was present and the outcome of the excavation would depend upon how well he was influenced by Shelley and Orna's proposals.

Shelley began the meeting, going over what they had learned about the boat during the preliminary excavation. Knowing a rough date for when the boat would have been in use on the lake, he stressed the importance of the boat for Christians, but also explained its importance for Israel's own interests, both secular and religious. No other ancient boat had ever been found in the Sea of Galilee despite efforts in the past, and Shelley made it quite clear that if this boat were not rescued soon, the only opportunity they were given to find such a treasure might slip away for good.

He made sure to point out the looming threat of treasure seekers, who would undoubtedly destroy the boat if the site were not protected and excavated as soon as possible. Avi listened to what Shelley had to say, and then the floor was turned over to Orna.

Orna explained to Avi and all the meeting participants that it would not be an easy task to save the boat from the mud. Because of its fragile, waterlogged state, great care would need to be taken to ensure that the timbers didn't dry out during the excavation. The dig would have to be fast, and once the boat was out of the mud, it would need to be preserved. Shelley says that her estimated budget for the full project was about $300,000.[1]

It took a while for Avi to come to a conclusion once the proposals had been presented. The boat certainly needed to be saved—it was a national treasure, and an archaeological and historical gem. But an emergency excavation with a budget of $300,000 was a lot to consider for a government bureaucracy without a lot of wiggle room in the budget. In the end, though, Avi agreed with everyone else. The excavation would begin in three days.

Given the O.K. to start the project, the archaeologists needed to assemble a skilled team to take on the monumental task set before them. Shelley was well connected in the archaeological world, and knew exactly who was needed for the project. The problem was, one of the most integral and necessary people to have on board the excavation was Dr. Richard Steffy. Steffy was the leading expert in ancient ship construction at the time, and as far as Shelley was concerned, if they couldn't have Steffy on the team they might as well not excavate the boat. Steffy, who passed away in December of 2007, co-founded the Institute of Nautical Archaeology and reconstructed ancient ships found in Greece, Turkey, and Italy. Shelley knew that the excavation needed him desperately—he was the best.

Unfortunately, he was in America and would need to fly to Israel to be part of the crew. Thankfully, he agreed to come and he said he would freely volunteer his time for the excavation. Shelley didn't want him to have any expenses for this trip, so he told Steffy that his plane ticket would be provided for him.

It seemed to the excavation team impossible to acquire the funding for his plane ticket, though. They already knew that the Department of Antiquities had quite a thinly stretched budget, and since it had agreed to put up the funding for the excavation, it was a long shot that the money for a last-minute transatlantic flight would be able to be freed up.

Previously, on another excavation, Kurt and Shelley had worked with some volunteers whose family members worked at the American Embassy in Israel. Shelley decided to try his luck and got in touch with one of his contacts at the embassy, hoping that the prior enthusiasm for archaeology had not burned out. He was put in touch with the American ambassador at the time, Thomas Pickering, who was himself quite fond of archaeology.

After speaking with the embassy, Shelley was unable to focus or get any work done. He knew the efforts of the excavation would be wasted if the funding couldn't come through—no one would be able to evaluate the boat as well as Richard Steffy, but it was out of his hands. After hours of waiting, Shelley couldn't handle it anymore. He called up the embassy to see if any decisions had been made. The funding for the ticket had already been approved.

With Richard Steffy on the way, it seemed as though the excavation could at last get going. Before they could start, however, a precedent would be set. It was beginning to seem that at each step of the way, the excavators were going to be faced with massive obstacles they'd need to overcome.

The date was Saturday, February 15, the day before the excavation was to begin. Shelley, knowing that preparations had to be made before the dig could start, went to Ginosar to discuss the plans with Moishele. After a day of work, they walked out to the beach to once again survey where the boat was hidden, buried under the mud.

There was a terrible surprise waiting for them when they arrived.

At the beginning of the whole process, when Kurt and Shelley had first arrived and pronounced the boat ancient, the water line of the Sea of Galilee had been almost 100 feet away from the boat site.

Since that day, with the rainstorm and double rainbow, the drought was broken. This was wonderful news for Israel—the water level of the Sea of Galilee was rising again, and it seemed there would be no shortage of water. Unfortunately, the news was not so wonderful for the excavation.

Although the archaeologists had initially hoped to wait a substantial length of time so that the excavation could be conducted under water, the gears had already been set in motion and they needed to rescue the boat quickly. All of the recent rains had raised the water level a good amount, and it was now within 30 feet of the boat. With more rain forecasted for the near future, the site would be flooded with water in no time.

A few feet of water around the boat would not afford the underwater excavation initially desired; it would only slow down the process and make an already almost impossible task even harder. Now that the archaeologists had had a chance to investigate the boat, they knew that too much exposure to the warm fresh water would allow bacteria to destroy the boat. Shelley and Moishele both knew that something needed to be done, or else the boat was going to be lost.

With everything on the line, the rescuers started to become desperate. Avi, the director of the Department of Antiquities, was going to be meeting the following day with Yitzhak Navon, the Minister of Education, a man whose signoff was needed for the final approval of excavation. Shelley decided to ask Avi to request a favor from Navon at their upcoming meeting.

On their way back from the beach, Moishele had come up with an interesting idea. Recalling the pumps of the National Water Carrier that supply water to the rest of the country, he suggested that a request be put in for enough water to be pumped out of the lake to ensure that the dig site remain dry.

Although it was a long shot, Avi agreed to speak with Navon

about the issue, and see if he would be willing to ask Arye Nehem-kin, then Minister of Agriculture, to pump water from the lake and lower the level.

With that matter up in the air, everyone tried to get some sleep and prepare for the start of the excavation the following day. All they could do was pray their request would be taken seriously.

Sunday, February 16 dawned, and the members of the excavation who were at Ginosar got ready to begin. Several members of the crew had not yet arrived, but work could be gotten underway before everyone was present. When the assembled group headed out to the excavation site, there were a couple of men who were interested in the discovery and wanted to ask Shelley a few questions.

The men were moshavniks from Migdal. A moshav is another kind of settlement in Israel, different from a kibbutz in that while a cooperative farming community, the land and farms are individually, rather than communally, owned.

The men were curious about the boat, and asked why it was so important. Shelley gladly explained that the boat held substantial religious and historical significance, and that since it was the only boat of its kind to ever be found in the Sea of Galilee, it was an invaluable discovery. He also told them that the excavators would need to be very careful as they worked on the boat because it was in an extremely fragile condition, and they would need to be painstakingly cautious to make sure it wasn't damaged.

What Shelley had to say made the Migdalites quite pleased.

They thanked him for explaining everything to them, and in turn explained to him that they had been wondering whether or not the boat should be displayed at Migdal. The stretch of beach that the boat was buried in lay across the road from Moshav Migdal. The Migdalites asserted that the boat had been found on their land, thus it rightfully belonged to them. Having been made aware of the precarious condition of the boat, they now knew that they could threaten to destroy the boat if their wishes were not complied with, and that was exactly the threat they made.

The men from Migdal informed the would-be excavators that, should they try to excavate the boat without an agreement stating that the boat would be displayed at Migdal, they would have no option but to destroy the craft. They did not want to let an opportunity like this escape, and they made it quite clear that if they could not have the boat, then no one could.

Predictably, this brought an abrupt halt to the entire operation.

Avi was in his office in Jerusalem that day, and the group wasted no time in informing him of this latest development. He made the only call available to him, and ordered the excavation stopped until the situation could be worked out. Immediately he was on the phone, trying desperately to get in touch with anyone at Migdal, but no one would respond to his efforts.

The situation came to a head when one of the kibbutz schoolteachers, with her class of kindergarteners in tow, approached Shelley to ask him why a man with a gun was standing guard over the boat. With loaded weapons being brought into the excavation site, the time to be diplomatic had passed. If the Migdalites were carrying guns around and refused to talk with Avi, the boat crew knew it was time to call the police.

The officers who arrived were also from Migdal, and knew the man with the gun. Nonetheless, heated words were exchanged, and the police ordered the man guarding the boat to stand down. With the authorities involved, the man finally put his gun away, and then everyone drove over to Migdal to sort the situation out.

In the room where they met, no one was happy with how things were going. The Migdalites had likely imagined agreement with their demand to come quickly and were flustered now that the police were involved. Their plan had not gone at all as they had envisioned.

Shelley forced one of the moshavniks to speak with Avi over the phone, though it was clear that none of them wanted to. In his book, Shelley does not record what the conversation between the man from Migdal and Avi consisted of, but he does say that the moshavnik quickly, though reluctantly, fell in line through the persuasion of the director of the Department of Antiquities.[2]

There is a good chance Avi may have explained what a trial such an excavation would be, with great expense and low chance of success. He probably did not know the extent of what the difficulties would be, but having years of experience in archaeology, he likely had a fair idea.

He may also have pulled rank as the director of the Department of Antiquities and told the man that he could easily have the government and military involved, which would not only ruin Moshav Migdal's plan, but also cause a fair amount of embarrassment. Regardless of what he said, the Migdalites changed their tune and grudgingly agreed not to cause any more problems with the excavation.

With one significant problem taken care of, the excavation was back on, but the team had no word on whether or not the government would lower the level of the Sea of Galilee to combat the threat of rising water. The excavation had already been delayed due to the Migdalite threat, and with Richard Steffy on the way later that week they had to get started so that he could have a chance to inspect the boat.

Kurt later said that there was a lot of fear that the water flooding the site would destroy the boat. For the most part the crew understood that, although they probably could not save the boat, they would at least have a chance to record and document it as the only ancient boat ever to be found in the Sea of Galilee.

I say most of the crew understood that, because two people on the team knew that the boat would survive. Moishele and Yuvi did not for a minute lose hope that they would be able to rescue the boat from the mud.

The excavators were determined to do everything they could to keep the boat from being destroyed. That determination, combined with the hope the Lufan brothers refused to let go of, kept the whole project afloat through countless ordeals. The excavation of the boat began that night.

3

STUCK IN THE MUD

By the time the disaster presented by the Migdalite situation had been defused, a significant portion of the day had been swallowed up. The team had expected to begin excavating the boat that morning, but now the afternoon was wearing on and no progress had been made. Everyone's nerves had been strained—even those who had not gone over to Migdal had been tested when they saw a hostile, armed man standing guard over their excavation site. Over the coming week and a half, their nerves wouldn't get any better.

On the first night of the excavation, everyone was in high spirits. At last, after weeks of waiting, the miraculous boat was finally going to be uncovered. Not even Yuvi, Moishele, Kurt, or Shelley had seen too much of the boat yet. In the preliminary dig, they had looked at the planking of the fishing boat, but they still hadn't dug down inside its hull to see what the interior of the boat looked like.

The work was far from easy. Shovels and other tools could be used to get out most of the mud, but they had to be kept away from the fragile timbers of the boat. One hasty scoop was all it would take for a massive chunk to be taken out of the boat's frame; with the wood in such a delicate condition, such damage would almost certainly be irreparable. As far as they knew, buried in the mud at their feet was a fairly intact ancient hull, and everyone wanted to keep it that way.

The only way to make sure no tools would gouge holes in the boat was to dig a significant amount of the mud out by hand. Had the boat been buried in normal, loose silt, the task would have been time consuming, but not terribly strenuous. The mud encasing the boat, however, was anything but loose. After nearly 2,000 years, the

Night falls on the excavation's first day

mud had been packed down firmly into place. On top of that, the mud was actually more clay than anything else.

On the first night of the dig, everyone was fairly fresh. It had been a trying day, and it was much later in the day than anticipated, but no one had done any heavy labor yet. They were able to dig through the muddy clay, if not easily, at least steadily. Regardless, the dense and heavy sediment packed around the boat painfully wore down on their fingers. At the end of a shift, the fingertips on the hands of anyone who had been digging were sore and raw. Each finger felt as though it had been dragged along sandpaper for however many hours had been spent digging.

Almost all of that digging was yet to come. On the first night of the excavation and throughout the whole ordeal, high spirits carried everyone far above where fatigue might threaten to drop them. Yuvi even said that he never felt tired during the whole process, although he was at the site as long as anybody else was. Along with the rest of the crew, he sacrificed sleep, running on only a few hours a day, and worked up to 16 hours each day trying to save the boat.

There were many reasons to work as quickly as they did. Initially, Shelley and Kurt knew they had to clear the boat as well as they could before Richard Steffy arrived at the site. If during the few days he was free to be on location they had nothing for him to look at, his trip would be a waste. Additionally, the rising waters were an ever-present threat. The long-prayed-for winter rains, insufficient for the past few years, were finally beginning to fall steadily. Every time it rained, the water poured into and around the Sea of Galilee, making the mud nearly as impossible to work in as quicksand. On top of that, rivers and streams that fed into the Sea of Galilee were flowing full again.

The water level of the Sea of Galilee was rising fast, and every time the excavators looked at it, its water was creeping closer and closer to the boat. On that first night of digging, the Department of

Antiquities had not yet supplied the crew with the equipment they would need for the excavation, so everything was improvised. With only makeshift sandbags, no one was sure how long the water would be held at bay. At that point, the hopes of the entire excavation were pinned on Minister of Agriculture Nehemkin approving the request to pump water out of the lake.

That request was granted. Sort of.

As midnight of the first day of excavation rolled around, a small group of officials from the Kinneret Authority arrived at the beach. Navon, the Minister of Education, had apparently passed the request on to the Ministry of Agriculture. Nehemkin, thinking that lowering the water level sounded like the best way to save the boat, passed a request on to the Kinneret Authority.

The director of the Kinneret Authority, Zvi Ortenberg, had received the request from Nehemkin. Ortenberg was incredulous that the message passed on to him from the Ministry of Agriculture was accurate. He assumed that, much like in a game of telephone, something had been heard or repeated incorrectly. Convinced of this, he and a few other men headed to the excavation site on the first night of digging to find out what the archaeologists actually wanted.

Once there, they met with Kurt and Shelley, and explained why they had come. After the necessary introductions, the conversation went something like this:

"Well, I got a message from the Ministry of Agriculture, but I'm fairly certain I heard it wrong. He asked that we lower the water level of the Sea of Galilee to help you out. What was it you actually wanted?"

"Actually, that's pretty much what we requested . . ."

Understandably, this put Ortenberg in a tricky situation. After such a long drought, it was imperative that they allow the Sea of Galilee to refill. If they started pumping water out now, there was a possibility that the rains would stop. With the heat of summer only a few months away, voluntarily lowering the Sea of Galilee did not seem like a good option.

That option wasn't even available to him. He explained that, due to the volume of water flowing in every day, and with the constant increase in the water level, even turning the pumps on to full capacity would not draw enough water out to save the boat. It would probably buy some time, but it was not an effective solution. While using the pumps was out of the question for this reason, there was something better that he could promise.

Ortenberg promised that in the morning, equipment in the forms of tractors, shovels, and sandbags would arrive on the site. Men from the Authority would be on hand to throw up sandbags and build a dike to prevent the rising water from submerging the ancient vessel. Kurt and Shelley thanked him and, finally feeling like they could successfully excavate the boat, returned to the mud and continued digging.

As the work progressed that first night, the excavators had to be careful not to expose too much wood. Orna was in Jerusalem and would not arrive until the coming morning. As the conservationist, it was imperative that she be able to see the wood of the boat before too much of it was exposed. It was up to Orna to determine how it needed to be treated during the excavation. Without her at the site, the diggers had to make sure they didn't completely remove its protective mud casing. That mud had preserved the boat for nearly two millennia, and no one wanted to expose its timbers to the elements without knowing what effects that would have.

With that delicacy in mind, the crew scooped away a fair amount of the mud within the boat, but left an earthen shell packed tightly to the wooden hull. However, so close and after so much anticipation, no one could wait until the morning to see if the hull actually was intact.

Following their curiosity, Shelley and a kibbutznik from Ginosar gingerly climbed into the boat and lay on their stomachs in the mud. It was a cold night, and the excavators' breath was visible in front of their faces, floating in the air like the clouds that had recently threatened to flood the dig site. Despite the cold and the groundwater soaking through their clothing, the two men carefully scraped mud away, clearing a hole down and anxiously awaiting the resistance of wood against their fingers.

Finally, they felt the bottom of the boat. Using the groundwater that was welling up around them, the two men gently washed the muddy wood clean, and then pulled back to let everyone see it.

An immediate hush fell around the site as each member of the team drew close to see the hull. There it was, at last. Bathed in the warm glow of fishermen's gas lanterns, the bottom of the boat looked clean and almost new. For the first time in almost two thousand years, one of the rib frames holding the planking together once again looked out on a cold Israeli winter night. Proof had at last been uncovered that the hull of the boat was indeed intact and had survived its long slumber in the mud.

Much as they would have loved to, the crew couldn't afford a lot of time to stand around and gaze at the beautiful sight. Being a proper archaeological excavation, there was a lot to do that depended on everyone's hard and focused effort. Both because it was dark out and because sufficient time was needed for the task, the mud dug out from the inside of the boat was collected in buckets and carted away.

Saving and preserving the boat was not the only thing to be done. Once the dig was completed and the boat had moved on to the conservation stage, archaeologists would need to thoroughly search through the mud and make sure that no potsherds or other artifacts had been missed in the frenzied excavation. These additional artifacts, like the oil lamp, could help provide key clues to the boat's life on the Sea of Galilee.

The first look at the boat's frame

However, before the mud could be investigated in detail, there was a lot of work to do on the boat. As the sun slowly asserted itself in the breaking dawn, it seemed as though the excavators might not have the chance to do that work after all. The growing light revealed what everyone had been afraid of—the waters of the Sea of Galilee were almost upon the work site.

The few improvised sandbags the kibbutz had managed to throw together were proving insufficient. The water had risen to their position on the beach, and if it rose any further it would soon sweep past them, inundating the site. To top this off, a breeze, indicating the beginning of a sharkia, began to blow across the lake down from the Golan Heights.

Most sharkias increase in power fairly quickly, and the crew from the Kinneret Authority had not yet arrived on the scene with the promised equipment. Without a sturdy dike built up of mud and sandbags, a strong sharkia would swamp the excavation and destroy any pieces of the boat already exposed.

Running out of time and ideas, Shelley took the matter into his own hands. He is an atheist, but at a desperate time like this he needed somewhere to put his faith, and fast. Moved by deepest necessity and urgency he stepped away from the boat and waded into the shallows of the Sea of Galilee. Waist deep in the rising water, Shelley lifted his hands in the air and prayed to the Sea of Galilee. He felt that it was time to ask permission from the lake to take the boat it had held onto for so long.

Shortly after Shelley's moment of spirituality, a low rumbling started to become audible. The tractors and equipment promised by the Kinneret Authority were driving down the beach.

The men from the Authority immediately set about throwing up an earthwork dike and stabilizing it with sandbags; the dike became the most important project. Visions of the boat lying in pieces blown across the beach filled the excavators' minds with horror. If

The dike is constructed behind the boat

the sharkia started howling ferociously before the dike was built, their dreams would be scattered down the beach along with the pieces of broken boat.

An adequate dike was completed before long, and a sigh of relief ran through the crowd of excavators. Now, not only was the threat from the sharkia dealt with, but also the danger posed to the boat by the rising water level would no longer be an issue. Because of the need to build dikes, Kurt, an immigrant from the Netherlands, later said that it felt like a Dutch excavation. The water level continued to rise, but the crew now had the proper materials they needed to ensure the size of the dike could be increased to keep out the water, no matter how high it rose.

Throughout the night and the early part of the day, the mud collected for further study had filled all of the buckets the workers had

Buckets were filled with mud for later inspection

brought to the site. Shelley and Kurt knew they needed to keep a record of the mud in case anything was found in it. Here, as in many other situations that would arise during the excavation, Kibbutz Ginosar came to the rescue.

As the crew lacked proper storage containers for the mud removed from the boat, large plastic crates were given for that purpose from the kibbutz's factory. With ample containers available for mud storage, Shelley requested that all of the mud from inside the boat and within the span of a meter from its frames be collected for storage and marked with what section it had been taken from.

The site had been plotted with piping driven into the soft earth. Utilizing these pipes, a makeshift grid had been created, dividing the dig into individual sections. Using this grid system, labels were affixed to the crates indicating the sections from which the contained mud had been taken. The crates were then loaded onto a forklift and driven back to the kibbutz for storage.

Picking up the crates with the forklift was easier said than done. The forklift tractor had prongs that were too wide to manipulate the plastic boxes, and wooden boards had to be tied onto the prongs in order to hold the crates up. Slipping in the soggy mud, workers had to manually lift the heavy crates and hoist them onto the boards. After an excess of effort, the tractor had its first of many loads ready to be driven back to the kibbutz.

One of the volunteers, Karen, the wife of assistant American ambassador under Thomas Pickering, agreed to follow the crates and make sure they were properly dumped. After so much work to get the labeled mud transported, it would be devastating if the crates were spilled or mismatched. By the time she returned with the tractor to the excavation, she found to her relief that the process had evolved into a smooth procedure.

That seemed to be the course of events for much of the excavation. For every need that cropped up, for which there seemed to be no solution, members of the crew would speak up and it turned out that they were perfectly suited for the task. The site photographer turned out to be one of the members working on the excavation, and one of the onlookers from the crowd became the dig's recorder.

It isn't terribly surprising that help should have come even from the crowd of people watching the boat's excavation. Although the initial group had tried to keep the discovery quiet, the excavation had become a media frenzy. Inevitably, along with the camera crews large crowds of tourists had showed up as well. In fact, this excavation proved to be one of, if not the best-recorded excavation in history. Within a few days of the outset of the excavation, twelve or thirteen television stations had crews on site filming the dig.

The excavation was going on during the time of the war with Lebanon, so the crews were already in the north of Israel. Now that there was finally something newsworthy going on other than the war, the stations jumped at the opportunity and sent their crews to film the dig. A biblical discovery, something positive and uplifting

Camera crews swarm around the boat

for the world to see broadcast from Israel, was a welcome change of focus from the constant reminder of an ongoing war. Day and night, the uncovering of the boat from the time of Jesus' life was under the scrutiny of the public eye.

From day one, the excavation site was simultaneously a tourist location. So many people wanted to come and see the boat that the Migdalites who had tried to claim the boat as their own saw part of their wish come true. Some of the moshavniks put up a barrier across the road and charged admission for anyone who wanted to visit the excavation site. Just behind the crowd of tourists, hot dog stands and ice cream vendors stood at the ready to cater to the tourists standing at the fence, watching the excavation progressing.

Because there were so many people at the site, there was a high level of security to make sure that nothing happened to the boat. A fence of police barriers was erected, and patrolling that fence were police officers, border guards, and soldiers from the Israeli army. The guards patrolling the site even had German shepherds watching over the boat. Many of the people at the site were initially watching the excavation because they believed a load of gold would be uncovered in the boat.

Once word spread that it was definitely not the Turkish boat but was in fact a boat from Jesus' time, even more people came to visit the site for its potential religious significance. The police and military presence had been brought to the site to protect the boat from any onlooker who might feel suddenly overwhelmed by greed and cross the barrier to try and take a souvenir. They had to make sure that the boat at least lasted long enough to properly be recorded, even if it wouldn't survive through conservation.

Orna arrived on the second day of the excavation, February 17. By the time she arrived at the site, a large amount of the mud inside the boat had been cleared out, but only the one patch of wood remained visible, the patch uncovered and cleaned by Shelley. The team was

The second day of the excavation

hesitant to remove the protective mud cocoon from the boat before Orna could tell them what would happen. It wasn't good news.

When she arrived, Orna of course wanted to see the boat, both from curiosity and from her desire to know how to handle the excavation. The rains and the rising water level had turned the beach into a soggy mud pit, and she had to make her way to the boat carefully. There wasn't a lot of exposed wood for her to see, and it seemed she would have to share what was available with Moishele. He was inside the hull with his hand in the muddy groundwater that filled the boat's bottom.

As he knelt there with his fingers pressed against the bare wood, nothing could have made him happier. For years he and his brother had been dreaming about this moment, and now he could actually touch his dream. Moishele wanted everyone to feel as happy as he did about the boat, so when he saw Orna approach, he took her arm and put it in the groundwater so that she could feel its planking as well.

Feeling the wood that first time told her volumes about the delicacy of the boat's situation. At first touch, she felt how soft and waterlogged the wood had become. She did not know at the time how thoroughly water had penetrated and replaced the cells in the boat's wooden frame, but one thing was clear: If it was left exposed too long, the water inside the boat would dry out and ruin an irreplaceable artifact.

At first, when Shelley and Kurt had felt the wood, they could tell it was heavily waterlogged. They had worked on dozens of shipwrecks and knew how drying out can affect the integrity of the ship's structure. When Orna explained to the whole crew what sort of issues they were facing with the excavation, neither Kurt nor Shelley was surprised by what she had to say.

The boat was being removed from the environment that had preserved it for about 2,000 years. It had been kept thoroughly wet and hidden away from the heat of the sun. The excavators who scraped the mud lining off the hull were potentially doing damage to the boat. They were taking away the moist environment to which it had become accustomed and replacing it with the direct heat of sunlight. This meant that before long, the wooden boat would begin to dry out irreversibly. Once the water inside the wood evaporated, the boat would lose all its strength. The individual pieces of wood would shrink and grow brittle, like dead leaves in autumn. After that, it was only a matter of time before the boat began to fall apart. Once that happened, the boat could not be put back together. If it were even worth it anymore, the only thing that could be displayed would be a collection of dry chunks that had originally been a boat.

Measures had to be taken to ensure that such a fate did not befall the boat. At first, a structure was rigged so that a piece of clear plastic sheeting could be set up over the site as a sort of tent, in order to keep the direct heat of the sun from ravaging the boat. The sheet was quickly taken down once it was realized that the hot, moist atmosphere underneath it would turn the ancient wood into a bacteria farm.

The second idea to keep the wood from drying out was not as easy as the plastic sheeting would have been, but it seemed to do the trick. While the excavation was going on, volunteers stood over the boat with spray bottles augmented by perforated garden sprinkler hoses, all in a desperate bid to keep the boat's waterlogged timbers as wet as possible. It wasn't a permanent solution, but for the time being, it was as good as the team could get. The race was on—the faster the boat could be excavated, the faster it could be submerged in water, which seemed the only way to save its fragile structure.

Keeping the boat constantly irrigated presented an additional problem for the crew. Now, in addition to the groundwater welling up where the mud was removed, more water was being sprayed into the hole. Although the boat needed to stay saturated, if the excavation pit was full of water, the excavators could not get their work done.

The Kinneret Authority once again came to the rescue and supplied the excavation with an additional set of tools—pumps. If you have ever dug a hole at a beach, you know that it is next to impossible to keep that hole dry. Even though the hole may be set back from the lake or ocean's visible water level, groundwater will still seep through the mud or sand, filling the hole up to the level of the water table.

Groundwater at the Sea of Galilee was doing the exact same thing with the excavation pit. While the groundwater around the boat wouldn't pose the same level of danger to the excavation as the lake's waves would, having a constant level of standing water in the dig site complicated the rescue process. Every extra complication meant more time until the boat could be treated in the conservation phase, which made the chances of rescuing the boat slimmer. The pumps the Kinneret Authority provided made sure there would be one less problem slowing the process down.

One more concern had been taken care of, but there were countless more facing the crew. As the excavation wore on over the days prior to Dick Steffy's arrival, the team knew that the different planks and frames of the hull needed to be differentiated and clearly labeled. This was a necessary task, because Steffy would have to look at the individual pieces of wood to get as thorough an idea of the boat's original construction as possible.

Danny Syon, a young archaeologist, had volunteered his time to help with the excavation in whatever capacity was needed. Claire Epstein, the archaeologist from Ginosar, had passed his name, along with his expressed desire to help, along to the excavators. Shelley knew exactly what Danny could do for them.

One of the many materials Ginosar had supplied for the excavation was a spool of white plastic cording. Shelley gave the cording to Danny and asked him to outline each individual piece of wood so that when Steffy arrived, his time could be maximized. Danny set about the process, carefully determining which breaks in the wood were cracks and which were seams between joints. Using the mortise and tenon peg heads as a guide, he started to define each timber separately, which when finished gave a fantastic glimpse of the boat's construction.

The cording could be wedged into the seams of the wood, but an effective method of affixing the string, as well as labels, to the ancient wood had yet to be determined. Often, in an excavation like

Danny's cording between the planks

this with a wood subject, small steel pins can be stuck in the wood. Such pins could be easily removed, and the tiny holes left by the pins would blend right in with the weather-beaten wood's natural grain. Because the crew had available to them a quantity of straight pins, they put them to use and pinned both the cord and labels to the boat.

In the moist wood and humid air, it didn't take long at all for the pins to begin rusting.

Once the rusting was noticed, Orna immediately felt the pins ought to be removed. The oxidation process corroding the pins could easily affect the planking. Because the wood was in such a delicate state already, everyone agreed that the fewer stresses placed upon the boat, the better off it would be. Without being able to use the pins, however, the boat might not be properly marked and labeled by the time Steffy arrived at the site. An alternative solution had to be found.

Quietly, Moishele provided the solution. The hot and dry climate in Israel provides the perfect environment for cacti to thrive in. Going back to the kibbutz, he found a needle-laden cactus in Ginosar's garden and stripped it of its needles. With a look of humble triumph on his face, he returned to the excavation and brought back a cupful of cactus needles. The needles couldn't last as long as the steel pins, because once waterlogged they became soft and droopy. Regardless, these biological pins provided a safe, albeit temporary alternative to their rusting counterparts.

To the excavators, it seemed as though for every problem they solved, two more cropped up. As everyone toiled away in the mud, the work became increasingly difficult. Although the problem of rising water had been taken care of, rain continued to fall on a consistent basis, and this made the muddy surface around the boat much more difficult to navigate.

Workers were up to their elbows in mud cleaning the shell away from the boat, and walking had to be done carefully, or else a foot might sink into the sediment. If you have ever walked through heavy mud, you know how challenging it can be to extract a foot that has been swallowed by a mud hole. Frequently, in such situations you can pull your foot free, but at the expense of leaving your shoe stuck in the same place. Even if your laces are tight and your foot comes away with your shoe still tied on, mud gets up over the tops of the shoe and spills down onto your foot.

Having to constantly extricate your feet from mud can be frustrating and tiring, and the excavators were tired enough as it was. Long hours in the mud and the sun wore down on everyone working on the dig, and they had to put in a grueling effort for almost two weeks of work. Many of them had obligations that they had to fulfill in addition to the work on the boat, and that left precious little time for sleep.

Kurt and Shelley, in particular, were running around with absolutely no time to spare. Back by the ancient city of Dor on the Mediterranean Sea, Kurt lived in Kibbutz Nahsholim. In each kibbutz, members are assigned certain responsibilities. It is because of this sharing of the workload that many of the kibbutzim have been successful in Israel. Even though Kurt was working on an important archaeological excavation, he was not exempt from his daily chores.

Every day, Kurt had to make the drive between Nahsholim and Ginosar, about 90 minutes each way. He had to go between excavating a boat that a month before no one would have believed existed, and milking cows and collecting chicken eggs. His fellow kibbutzniks at Nahsholim didn't care about the boat he was working on—if he didn't get his chores done, he would be kicked out of the kibbutz.

Because the excavators were working day and night, they had to take breaks during their shifts to rest. As lead archaeologists on the site, however, Kurt and Shelley had to use their breaks to drive into Herzliya, near Tel Aviv, to give lectures and presentations in the American Embassy. The Department of Antiquities could not get the funding for the excavation together in such a short amount of time, so the presentations the two archaeologists gave at the embassy were primarily to large corporations, trying to get either monetary donations or, typically, donations of materials desperately needed to complete the excavation.

Without giving these presentations, the team would not have had the resources necessary to properly excavate and save the boat. However, the extra time required by these meetings left the archaeologists dangerously sleep deprived. Finally, at the dig site, the lack of sleep took its toll.

Suffering from extreme fatigue, Shelley collapsed one day while working on the boat. A tent had been erected nearby, so some of the workers carefully lifted him off of the mud and carried him into the tent, out of the sunlight. Now, the excavators were at a loss for what to do. Kurt and Avi Eitan, the director of the Department of Antiquities, met to discuss what they should do. Shelley clearly needed to rest—as they all did—but he was an integral part of the excavation. Should they replace him? Should they just give him some time to recuperate?

Thankfully, all that he needed was a bit of rest to recover from his collapse. He wound up all right, and was able to return to work on the boat before too long. However, his fainting spell set an ominous pall over the excavation. Everyone was working long, exhausting hours during the day in the hot Israeli sun. The labor was intense, and it wasn't hard to imagine others coming down with severe exhaustion or heatstroke by the time the excavation was completed.

The long hours weren't the only part of the excavation that

was hard on the body, though. As the dig progressed and more of the boat was freed from its mud cover, its weak timbers lost the support that had held them in place for 2,000 years. Orna tried to prop it up with some flat pieces of wood, but the hull had the structural integrity of wet cardboard nonetheless. If anyone working on the inside of the boat put any pressure onto its fragile timbers, it would give way and that section of the boat, if not more, would collapse.

Because of the boat's fragility, once the mud wall supporting the boat from the outside had been removed, nobody could kneel in the boat to remove the interior mud casing. Everyone who had work to do on the inside of the boat, both those digging and Danny labeling, had to stand around the sides of the boat and lean in without putting any weight on the frame.

Bending over for several hours at a time is a true test of endurance. Even leaning over a low table for twenty minutes can put strain on one's back. Everyone who had to work on the boat's interior after the natural mud supports had been removed was forced to stand in this position, bent over double at the waist, in order to reach down to the bottom of the inside of the boat.

On top of that, most of those doing such work had to be lifting heavy, wet mud out of the hull. At the end of each such shift, the workers would barely be able to straighten up and stand tall—their backs were just too sore. It felt as though their backs had been crunched in half. There wasn't really an alternative to the situation, though. Until the boat's interior could be emptied, cleaned, and labeled, the delicate work had to continue.

A couple of days after the dig started, someone finally came up with a pain-free solution.

Two towers had been constructed for the excavation site, originally built as platforms from which to oversee the dig from an unobstructed vantage point. By the time everyone working on the boat's interior seemed to be suffering from back pain, Moishele decided that the towers could be put to better use. He got a volunteer from the kibbutz who was a skilled welder, and the two men set about converting the towers into a more useful structure.

What resulted from their endeavor was a single, "bridging" structure that spread across the boat. From this contraption, cables were suspended and attached to wooden planks. The planks, in turn, presented a floating ledge, hanging directly above the boat once the structure was put into place. Workers could now lie on the ledge, suspended in mid-air above the boat, and scoop out the load of mud and clay that still sat in the boat's hull.

This piece of equipment proved to be invaluable. Not only did it provide a way for the excavators to clean the inside of the boat without applying pressure to its feeble timbers, but also it allowed

Excavators dig from the hanging platform

them to work for hours at a time without feeling the strain of the effort in their backs. Additionally, the structure provided a place from which to hang perforated irrigation hose, keeping the boat damp without requiring any of the volunteers to stand at the ready with spray bottles.

Although a lot of attention went to the cleaning of the boat's interior, a lot of commotion was being made at another part of the dig. At first, the boat had been beneath the level of the mud. That is, of course, how it was preserved, and how it was discovered. During the excavation, the mud around the boat was being removed, and so the boat started to rest above the mud around it. After a few days of digging, it had become awkward and difficult to dig along the sides of the boat and around its underside.

To make it easier to work on the exterior of the boat, the trench that had been dug around it needed to be widened. Once enlarged, it would allow the workers to stand beneath the level of the boat, while it was raised on a "pedestal" of mud. To widen the trench as efficiently as possible, a backhoe was brought to the site to dig out the mud.

Using the backhoe rather than shovels meant that the process could go much more quickly. Unfortunately, the greater volume of mud removed at an accelerated speed meant that it would be more difficult to ensure that the machine wouldn't destroy any auxiliary artifacts in the mud. Because the accidental destruction of additional artifacts was a possibility, a small number of the excavators had to check the mud being scooped out by the mechanical shovel. This slowed down the operation, but proved to be the right decision.

Zvika Malach was one of those men checking the shovel-loads of mud. Up to his elbows in mud, he made a startling and heart-stopping discovery. There were more wood fragments in the mud.

The section of the site being widened by the backhoe was a few yards from where the boat rested. The backhoe certainly hadn't taken any pieces off of the boat, so were there simply more pieces to the boat, perhaps parts that had fallen off years before?

This was something that needed to be investigated in detail. Some of the workers began searching the area where the shovelful of mud had been scooped. As they searched, Zvika suddenly cried out. As he knelt, digging in the muddy groundwater collecting in the site, he felt a piece of wood as weak and waterlogged as the rest of the boat. The backhoe was shut down and the only sounds came from the crowd as all the work stopped and everyone gathered around to see what Zvika had discovered.

When the water and mud had been removed, two additional pieces of frame and planking could be seen clearly, resting at the bottom of the pit. There was a chance that these newly exposed pieces of wood were parts of other boats—maybe even additional complete hulls, still buried underneath the surface of the mud. Regardless of where these pieces came from, the team couldn't just abandon them there.

Zvika was a moshavnik who lived at Migdal. This new, secondary discovery, since a Migdalite made it, finally united the moshavniks and the kibbutzniks on the excavation. Although there had been plenty of rivalry in the past between the two settlements, they all agreed that saving the boat was the most important goal ahead of them.

Moshavniks from Migdal now came to the site in greater numbers than before, and they were more than willing to help in any capacity needed. Although the additional wood fragments that Zvika found turned out to be only fragments and not additional boats, the greatest part of his discovery was that it created a bond between the members of the rival settlements. That development, while wonderful in terms of the relationship between the two groups, was part of the reason why the excavation could have been completed in such a short amount of time. No matter how many new volunteers came to the site, there was always work for them. It turned out to be an enormous blessing that the moshavniks volunteered to join the dig, because there remained many days of unfinished work.

4

$\mathcal{D}$

OUT TO SEA

Because of all of the willing laborers volunteering at the excavation, the project was kept moving at a feverish pace. Four days into the dig, hundreds of pounds of mud had been cleared away from the site, and almost the entire interior of the boat was free from its mud cocoon. The loss of so much mud had, however, taken a serious toll on both the boat and the group of workers.

When the heavy mud and clay sediment had been taken out of and away from the outer sides of the boat, the waterlogged planks were left without any support. While Orna had used some flat planks of wood to brace the hull, the ancient wood was losing its structural integrity as the water within it evaporated in the sunlight day after day. The wood was fighting to hold together, but after almost 2,000 years, it was running out of strength.

Everyone working watched the boat in horror as a section of the hull began to buckle and collapse. Workers rushed to the side of the boat and held the planking in place, striving against the inevitable. The archaeologists already knew that once the wood's watery structure had evaporated, there was no way of replenishing the water. As with an overcooked steak, there is no way to make it juicy again after it has dried out.

Helpless to do anything to fix the collapsed stern section, they made the decision to remove the fallen piece of planking and keep it separate from the boat. The loss of the segment of wood left the group feeling rather poorly. Orna's concerns about the boat being structurally sound enough to save started to seem sadly accurate. Perhaps the boat couldn't be rescued. Maybe Kurt was right, that the blessing here was that a boat had been found and archaeologists had been given a chance to document it. Maybe photos and knowledge would be the only things salvaged from this shipwreck after all. Even Yuvi was sensing a creeping feeling that now, after seeing his dream almost fully realized, it would be snatched away from him.

He didn't pay any attention to that creeping feeling, though. He and Moishele trusted that the boat would not have been revealed to them if it were just going to fall apart. Even if everyone else doubted, they knew that the boat would survive the excavation.

This collapse, and the fear that another, even more devastating catastrophe would befall the boat, had been the motivating factors behind the construction of the hanging platform Moishele built to assist the excavation of the boat's interior. Although he and his brother trusted that the boat would survive, they knew that they needed to do everything they could to make that happen. It may have survived on its own for two millennia, but now it had been put into the hands of the excavators.

Although everyone's spirits had sunk extremely low following the collapse, they were about to get a large boost. The night after the stern section gave way, professor Richard Steffy arrived at the excavation site. Steffy was a ship reconstructor, which means that he was able to look at the boat and learn all about the conditions faced by the shipwright, the tools used to build the boat, and possibly even how many different craftsmen had originally made the boat.

Steffy had recently worked with a boat found at Herculaneum, one of the Roman cities destroyed when Mount Vesuvius erupted in 79 A.D. Because of the high-caliber work he had done with that boat, the archaeologists knew that Steffy was the man to have for the Galilee boat. The lights were put on the boat and a hush fell over the workers as they gave the distinguished professor a chance to look over its delicate frame.

After a few minutes of scrutiny, he came back to give them his personal pronouncement: "Yep. You've got an old boat."

Was that it? Had Richard Steffy been flown to Israel at a moment's notice just to confirm what Yuvi and Moishele had known from the moment they laid eyes on the boat? The team working on the vessel's excavation had been waiting for some illuminating identification of the boat being from a particular period or a specification of the boat's purpose. Sure, verification from a reputable scholar was always a welcome thing, but this simple statement was more than a little underwhelming.

Regardless of what the excavators had hoped to hear—and they may not even have known what they expected him to say—Steffy was staying on the site for a few days, and didn't want to rush to make any hasty proclamations. As it turns out, he made the right decision waiting to say anything in detail about the boat. Truth be told, he was underwhelmed himself when he actually saw the vessel.

From his initial perspective, it certainly wasn't anything to look at. It looked, at first, like Dr. Frankenstein had built the boat. Many of the planks were not actually whole pieces of wood—they were smaller planks joined together to form something with a manageable size. Steffy didn't want to rush to any conclusions on the boat mainly because his immediate conclusions were negative. It seemed to him as though the boat's builder had no idea what he had been doing. In order to be fair, both to the ancient shipwright and to the modern excavators, he held his tongue until he had spent a few days studying the boat and could deliver an educated statement on it.

While Steffy was looking over the boat, the priority for the excavators was to give him the best view of its timbers as they could. In the first days immediately following his arrival, the remainder of the mud packed into the boat's interior was removed as quickly as possible. Having already lost one segment of the boat's planking, the team of workers was determined not to let any more pieces fall off. The wood was cleaned with all the delicacy the task afforded, and the wood was constantly being soaked with water to deter the evaporation of the water within the wood.

Once the interior of the boat had been just about emptied, a new question arose for the excavators: "Now what?"

Orna already knew how the boat was going to be conserved. In previous excavations involving ancient wood, a synthetic wax substance called polyethylene glycol, or PEG, had been used as a preservation material. In cases like this, PEG takes the place of the water in the boat's timbers—it soaks into the cellular structure, replacing the water. Because the PEG won't evaporate, it creates a permanent "waterlogging" situation.

The method of preservation with PEG had been used previously: on a Swedish warship, the *Regalskeppet Vasa;* and on a ship salvaged from the waters off the coast of Kyrenia, Greece. Each time, a different style of preservation had been adopted. The Vasa had been pulled out of salt water entirely intact, having sunk just moments into her maiden voyage. Because of her size, the Vasa could not be preserved through immersion in PEG, so the conservators sprayed the wax onto the boat's timbers over a period of 17 years. Once the spraying process was completed, it took an additional nine years of slow drying to complete the preservation.

The method of preservation used in the case of the Kyrenia ship was more likely to be adopted for the boat saved from the Sea of Galilee. Being a smaller boat, the Kyrenia ship was carefully recorded and then dismantled. The pieces of wood that constituted the ship were then put into a pool filled with PEG, allowing the wax to soak into the timbers. The immersion process used for the Kyrenia ship took much less time than the spraying method employed with the Vasa. Because it took less time, it would cost less money, and with funding from the Department of Antiquities uncertain, immersion in PEG was the method of choice for the Galilee boat.

This posed a problem, however. In order to follow the method used by the conservators of the Kyrenia ship, the excavators of the Galilee boat would have to dismantle it down to its individual planks, or at least small enough pieces to be manageable. The more time they spent working on and looking at the boat, though, the more they realized that the boat could not be taken apart.

The wood was in such a fragile state that there was a high likelihood any attempt at dismantling the boat would destroy it completely. The ancient wood had lost its inherent strength, and the pressure required to separate the mortise and tenon joints could leave the planks crumbled in the excavators' hands. Even if the wood was successfully pulled apart, there remained another, uncontrollable element of danger. What if, during the conservation process, the shape or size of the wood changed, even slightly, and the planks wouldn't fit back together to reconstruct the boat?

There were too many possibilities for devastating failure if the boat were dismantled. That meant that the only option open to the team was to conserve the boat in its entirety. Predictably, conserving the boat whole opened up yet another can of worms. If the boat was too fragile to take apart, then it was probably too fragile to move as well. If they couldn't take the boat apart, and if they couldn't move it either, what on earth were they supposed to do?

Desperate for a solution, Shelley worked the phones and called everyone in Israel he could think of who might be able to help. He called engineers, the army, and colleagues, willing to hear what anyone had to say. His requests for assistance brought a swarm of new faces to the excavation site, each eager to help.

The suggestions posed by the new visitors to the site ranged from the simple (using inflatable cushions to raise the boat) to the extravagant (building a new museum on location, leaving the boat in place). The myriad suggestions received were unique and innovative, but they all had one thing in common: None of them would work. Some of the proposals were too expensive and poorly thought out, and some of them had too great a chance of destroying the boat. After the eager newcomers had left, taking their suggestions with them, the excavation crew was back at square one.

Although it looked as though the project might be sunk after days of tireless physical labor, there was one chance to save the boat that popped up in two people's minds. Moishele had in the recent past worked on the kibbutz's chicken coops, and one of the tasks he had performed in that job had been insulating the roofs of the coops so the chickens wouldn't get cooked before they were supposed to. He had used polyurethane foam, the kind that comes now in spray cans for do-it-yourself home insulation projects. Moishele thought they might be able to envelop the boat in a polyurethane coating.

Orna had had the same idea as the fisherman. When she had originally come to the excavation site, Orna had brought with her small amounts of various materials she thought might prove useful to the project. The polyurethane she had brought had been used to fill the stern section of the boat, in a desperate bid to provide stability and ward off a collapse. While it had been too late for the stern section of the boat that had broken off, the rest of the boat still remained to be saved. Orna thought there was a chance the same technique could be used across the whole boat. But even this idea did not come without problems.

First of all, Orna had used what polyurethane she had brought to the site. It would take vast quantities of the material to provide a cocoon sufficient to protect the boat's frame from damage in transit, and neither Orna nor the archaeologists knew where they could obtain the necessary quantity of polyurethane on such short notice. Additionally, polyurethane alone would not provide adequate support for the boat. The weight of the entire package, between the wooden hull and the polyurethane covering, might easily fall apart because of all the weight. Additional supports, made of fiberglass and polyester, would be needed to make sure the whole thing didn't snap like a Popsicle stick. To top it all off, in the chemical process that turns the liquid polyurethane into a solidifying foam, a great amount of heat is given off. The heat created by this reaction could easily become yet another possible cause of irreparable damage to the boat.

There wasn't a lot of time to come up with different ideas for the transportation of the boat, though. With every additional hour of every day the boat was left exposed to the sun and open air, the waterlogged timbers dried out more. A decision had to be made fast, and it looked like the only two options were either encasing the boat in polyurethane foam or letting it dry out and disintegrate as it lay in the mud. Even though it was a long shot, the green light was given to cover the boat with polyurethane.

Once the decision had been made, the difficulties presented by the use of polyurethane foam were quickly overcome. Two kibbutzniks at Ginosar, David Ronen and Yohai Abbes, were the ones in charge of

David and Yohai start putting on fiberglass frames

maintaining the boats used by the kibbutz. In this job, they had become proficient in the use of fiberglass, and could easily manipulate it to provide "ribs" for the boat, both inside and out. Also, to protect the boat from both the heat of the "foaming" process of the polyurethane and from the resin used to harden the fiberglass, thin painter's sheets of polyethylene were laid down over the boat's frame.

It took three days to finish laying down fiberglass ribs inside the boat, during which time the workers finished cleaning out all the sediment from the interior of the hull. The workers had hastened their already fast pace as the two kibbutzniks hurried to get the boat supported as soon as possible. During those three days, a construction firm had been contracted to fill the boat with polyurethane.

Another member of Ginosar had come through in the clutch to connect the archaeologists with the firm. He had worked with them to insulate a building on the kibbutz's land, and hearing the need for polyurethane foam, he was quick to bring them into the project.

On the same night that the fiberglass frames had been finished, a man from the construction firm was on the site, ready to begin spraying the boat. He came equipped with two large tanks of liquids, the elements that when combined would create the foam. Each tank fed its contents through a hose, and the two hoses met in the handle of a gun that would spray the substance onto the polyethylene sheeting covering the interior of the boat.

The process that creates the polyurethane is similar to the process that creates epoxy glue. When making epoxy adhesive, two liquids are used. They are kept separated because, while by themselves they don't do anything special, when combined they form an incredibly strong bond. If they were kept mixed together, the entire solution would harden. The two polyurethane elements thus had to be kept in separate tanks.

Before the spraying process could begin, the excavators had to place PVC piping upright in the boat. Once the polyurethane foam was on the boat, it would be impossible to remove it without having to cut it all off. As the wood planks of the boat were so waterlogged, there was a strong chance that groundwater would rise up through the wood and begin to fill the boat with water from beneath. The pipes went through the polyethylene sheeting so that hoses could be lowered down to pump out any water that seeped in.

The fiberglass frames are completed

The polyurethane foam is sprayed onto the boat

The man with the spray gun stepped onto the platform hanging from the rig Moishele built and stood directly over the boat. As he stood above the boat, armed with a spray gun and illuminated by the lanterns pointed at the site, he must have looked as though he was about to destroy the boat. To an outsider, it would have seemed that was the case as he began to spray the ancient timbers with an orange liquid that looked like it was growing of its own accord.

As the liquid grew, it bubbled and developed into a lumpy, yellowish-orange foam that spread all over the boat's interior. The high performance equipment the construction firm provided allowed the foam filling to be completed all in one night. By the time the man was done spraying, the boat's interior was no longer visible, covered instead by a lumpy foam that had grown so much it almost swallowed up the hanging platform, as well.

Having got that finished—it was probably one of the fastest stages of the excavation, too—the worker from the construction firm was dismissed for the night. The team still needed to figure out how they were going to package the outside of the boat in the foam, but after a long few days of working at breakneck speed to get the interior of the boat cleared, it was time for some well-earned rest.

Arriving at the site the following morning, the crew were aghast at what they found. As they had feared, groundwater had welled up into the bottom of the boat. There was so much water that it had pushed the foam up, and the polyethylene sheeting was subsequently floating on top of the water in the hull. Hoses were lowered down the pipes that the excavators had the foresight to have installed in the foam, and sump pumps drew the water out of the boat.

To prevent this from recurring, hours were spent laboriously removing the polyurethane coating from the boat and exchanging the polyethylene sheet underneath it for a thinner one. Hopefully, with less material between the wood and the foam, the latter would grip more tenaciously to the frame of the ancient vessel. With that done, polyurethane was once again sprayed into the boat's interior. For an added measure of caution, the backhoe was brought back in to deepen the pit around the boat. They wanted to make sure that no more groundwater could seep into the boat.

Now that the boat was properly filled with foam, the archaeologists turned their minds to the next problem before them: How do you envelop a fragile hull in polyurethane foam without moving it? The boat could not be rotated to expose the hull's bottom, and besides, its exterior was for the most part still covered in mud.

Once again, the perfect solution popped into someone's head at the right time.

Because the boat needed to be kept steady, the mud beneath it had to be left in place. It had supported the boat for hundreds and hundreds of years, and the rescuers knew they couldn't remove the pedestal under the boat without causing irreparable damage to the frame. In order to leave the mud, for the most part, in place and supporting the boat, tunnels were dug underneath its keel, one at a time.

Each tunnel was very small, only wide enough to allow a single person to fit through on his stomach. The tunnels were dug by hand, with the exposed wood of the boat directly above the tunneler. The tunnels were dark and wet, and to this point, digging each tunnel was the most difficult and trying part of the excavation. It was certainly not a task for anyone with claustrophobia.

After each tunnel was completed, more plastic sheeting was laid—both on the mud, to keep it from being absorbed into the polyurethane, and on the frame of the ship, so David and Yohai could put rigid fiberglass ribs on to provide additional support. After the men finished attaching the fiberglass frames, polyurethane was sprayed on, filling the hole and creating a foam support to keep the boat steady.

Over the course of three days, tunnels were steadily being dug and filled in, slowly replacing the boat's original brown cocoon of mud with one of bright, orange foam. Looking back today, the process seems sterile and almost easy. At the time, it was anything but. The tunnelers spent hours each day for three days lying on their stomachs with muddy water seeping into their clothing.

It took two people to make a single tunnel, each digging from the

Tunnels underneath the boat

opposite side of the boat and meeting in the middle. They had to be precise in their digging; the tunnels were made as thin as possible so as to keep the boat free from additional strain. Because the tunnels were so thin, each scoop of mud could not be simply passed back out of the tunnel. Whoever was digging needed to scoot backwards out of the tunnel to dump his handfuls of mud before he could continue.

Needless to say, this was an extremely tiring process. On top of the physical labor required by the task, there was now an additional problem for the workers—the noxious smell of chemicals. Between the polyurethane and the materials used to form the fiberglass ribs, the site was becoming more and more difficult to work in.

Thankfully, on the third day of tunneling, the job was completed. There were no setbacks in this stage; it had merely been an exhausting undertaking.

The boat, or rather the huge mass of polyurethane foam that had swallowed the boat, stood in the center of the pit, bathed by sunlight and in the eyes of dozens, if not hundreds, of spectators. With the polyurethane successfully sprayed onto the boat, there was no longer an immediate threat of the wood drying out. The foam cocoon

The boat is fully encased in polyurethane

would insulate the boat, keeping it cool and damp, away from the heat of the Israeli sun. While the boat was now safe from drying out, at least for the time being, there still remained the task of bringing it to the museum.

Although the polyurethane protected the ancient ship to a degree, any high levels of stress placed upon the yet fragile object could still break it. This is why the team of excavators faced such a dilemma when they brainstormed a way to transport the boat.

Someone suggested using a helicopter; the Israeli Air Force had volunteered one of its own for the purpose. This seemed like a good idea at first, because it would probably be the most expedient method of transport. The polyurethane casing could be hoisted into the air by cables and flown down the beach to the museum in a matter of minutes. The only problem was, there was no guarantee of the boat's safety. The vibration caused by the aircraft's motor spinning its rotors could possibly splinter the boat, even if it left the polyurethane cover intact.

This was also a consideration when it came to using ground transportation. A truck carrying the boat would have to crawl along the beach as slow as possible so that neither the vibration of the engine nor any bumps in the "road" would rattle the aged timbers. However, it seemed as though using a truck was the best, if not the only, option available.

Because of the size of the boat, especially once enveloped in the polyurethane foam, the crew would have to use a flatbed truck to transport it. Here, predictably, they hit yet another snag. Flatbed trucks are not light. With the beach still a muddy quagmire, it was only too likely that the truck would sink into the mud, much as the military truck had done that had led Moishele and Yuvi to discover the boat in the first place.

So that the truck carrying the boat wouldn't be left with its wheels spinning in the mud, the excavators decided that a road would have to be laid down. Building a road was not going to be quick, easy, or cheap. Materials had to be provided, equipment needed to be brought out, people had to log even more hours of intense physical labor, and it would take a long time to build a sufficiently sturdy road on such a soggy base.

Once again, as the crew was stuck in a difficult situation with a hard decision to make, someone unexpectedly supplied the perfect solution. It would be relatively fast, easy, and cheap as well. The answer to the problem was so simple, it was astounding that no one had thought of it yet. They were trying to move a boat, right? Why not just "sail" it to the museum?

The rising water level that had initially been a deadly threat to the excavation's success had turned into its salvation. Amazingly, the specific events that had transpired during the course of the dig had provided the team with a natural solution to one of their never-ending problems. To keep the water out, a dike had been built between the excavation site and the Sea of Galilee. Pumps had been supplied to remove any water that seeped in through the mud, to keep the site dry. Additionally, a large pit had been dug around the boat, for the same purpose—keeping the groundwater at bay.

The icing on the cake came when the excavators decided to use polyurethane foam for the boat's protection. In addition to insulating the wood, keeping it damp and cool, the foam had one other important attribute. It floated! The Yigal Allon Museum sits right on the waters of the Sea of Galilee, so all the rescuers needed to do was flood the pit where the boat rested and float it over to the museum.

As had happened so frequently throughout the excavation, the equipment needed to complete the task at hand was supplied by donation to the site. A steam shovel was brought to the beach for the purpose of breaking down the dike wall to join the excavation pit to the lake. Before that could be done, the pit needed to be filled back up with water so that the force of a wave rushing in as the shovel breached the dike wouldn't damage the boat. The pumps that the Kinneret Authority had provided came in handy yet again.

The order was given to reverse the pumps, and soon they were spitting water from the Sea of Galilee into the excavation site. As the water level within the pit rose—a tedious process—slabs of mud sheared off the sides of the pit into the murky water. At the same time, the steam shovel scooped away the mud that had been used to build the dike, making sure to leave a barrier wall thick enough to keep the lake from flooding the hole before the water within the site had risen to the level of the water in the lake. With the excavation so close to completion, no one wanted anything to rock the boat. A premature rush of water could wipe out everything they had worked so hard to preserve over the past days.

There was concern that the boat wouldn't float properly in the water. For one thing, it had been nearly 2,000 years since the vessel had sailed in the Sea of Galilee. On top of that, the polyurethane could easily give the boat buoyancy quite different from its own. Not knowing how the boat would sit in the water, Orna clambered on top of the mass of polyurethane to lend some stabilizing weight to the whole package.

As she sat atop the boat, the water level rose high enough to raise the boat from the mud. The polyurethane casing bobbed in the water, its buoyancy lifting the ancient fishing boat off of the mud that had held it in place for almost two millennia. Everyone's eyes were fixed on the boat as the water finished filling up the pit. Once the water level was about the same as it was in the lake, the word was given to the steam shovel operator to breach the dike. As soon as his shovel broke through the retaining wall, the water from the Sea of Galilee immediately equalized the water level in the pit.

It was now the steam shovel's job to free the boat. It dug away at the remainder of the dike, opening up a hole between the pit and the lake large enough for the boat to fit through. One of the men from the Kinneret Authority, on hand to supervise the use of the pumps, stuck a measuring stick into the newly created channel to check if it was deep enough for the boat to clear it. Once the water was deep enough in the channel, it was time to re-launch the boat.

Eager to be a part of this historical moment, members of the excavation waded through the water, guiding the boat out of its personal harbor and into the lake. Everyone's hearts stopped momentarily—the bottom of the polyurethane casing caught on an underwater mud bank. The workers guiding the boat carefully dislodged it, making sure not to jostle it. After that point the boat was free and clear, and the people guiding it brought it out to "sail" for one last time in the Sea of Galilee!

Although they had been able to walk the boat out into the lake, it would be a difficult enterprise to walk the boat all the way down the shore to the museum. The water of the Sea of Galilee is heavy with silt and mud, and walking in water waist- to chest-high is about as easy as walking with weights around your legs and ankles. A group of teenagers from Kibbutz Ginosar decided to come to the rescue: They came from the kibbutz's harbor in a rowboat. They tied a tow-

The Sea of Galilee flows through the breached dike

With Orna riding, the boat sails on the Sea of Galilee once again

rope from their boat to the polyurethane-enveloped fishing vessel and, like a tugboat, towed the ancient boat into the harbor at Ginosar.

It had been eleven days since the excavation began: eleven frantic, exhausting, and demanding days. On the one hand, it seemed to everyone who had worked on the boat that it had been a much shorter period of time since they had started. On the other, with everything they had had to do, it seemed as though eleven days was too short a time to have completed such an intense dig. Regardless, there was a lot to be grateful for.

The excavation, which hardly anyone had believed could have been completed successfully, was over. Unorthodox was an understated way to describe the process, but everything had come together and worked out better than any of the experts had thought possible. True, there was a long phase of conservation ahead for the boat, but for now, the weary excavators could relax. That night, they would get the best night's sleep they had gotten in a long time. Everyone went to bed worn out, but satisfied.

———

That night, the boat was moored in the harbor. While everyone slept, it passed the night floating alongside other boats, just as it had done almost 2,000 years earlier.

MATTHEW 4: 18–22

The Cost of Following Christ

While walking by the Sea of Galilee, he saw two brothers, Simon (who is called Peter) and Andrew his brother, casting a net into the sea, for they were fishermen. And he said to them, "Follow me, and I will make you fishers of men." Immediately they left their nets and followed him. And going on from there he saw two other brothers, James the son of Zebedee and John his brother, in the boat with Zebedee their father, mending their nets, and he called them. Immediately they left the boat and their father and followed him.[1]

When Jesus approached the first four disciples, he found them hard at work. Two of them were fishing, which is not surprising considering their vocation. The other two were not fishing at that moment but mending their nets with their father—no less important a task than fishing.

These four men were fishermen, people whose lives depended on what they could draw from the sea. They were most likely poor and probably just managed to get by on what they earned from their daily catches. Most importantly, these men did not simply have themselves to consider. Zebedee, the father of James and John, is mentioned by name in this passage. He was surely the leader of his household, but his sons worked alongside him in his boat. It isn't clear whether or not James and John lived at home or if they had families of their own, but one thing is certain: They had people depending on them.

The family business for these brothers was fishing. Their father brought home money and food through this work, and the help of his sons was a huge windfall for him. Having two strong, able-bodied helpers meant that he did not have to hire laborers, effectively giving the family more food on the table.

Simon Peter was in the same situation. Elsewhere in the Gospels (Matthew 8:14) his mother-in-law is mentioned, which leads us to believe that he was married, or at least had been at one time. In the social environment of the first century, it was his responsibility to help care for his mother-in-law, even if his wife had died. What he made each day was spent not just on his own provisions, but hers as well (and perhaps those of others).

When Jesus came on the scene, these men left their work behind. While it might have seemed a nice break for them to take a few weeks off and travel the countryside, they were not planning on returning to work. They left for good, and in so doing left their families to continue living without them.

Peter and Andrew, in the middle of a day of fishing, left their boat and nets, their most valuable possessions, in order to follow Jesus. James and John not only left their nets behind, they got up and left their father behind them. These men made an incredible sacrifice—they literally left their livelihoods behind them so that they could follow after Jesus, even before they knew who he was.

Remember that this was at the beginning of Christ's ministry in Galilee—he had only just recently been tempted by the devil in the wilderness, and was just starting out his mission of redemption. These four fishermen recognized something extraordinary about Jesus and were drawn by what he had to say. There probably wasn't much of a crowd around him at this point—there wasn't anything flashy about this Nazarene at all.

The call of God touched these men in the middle of their busy lives, interrupting their plans and their routines. They were so receptive to His voice that they left everything, possessions and family, in order to obey. Not only that, but they left and followed Jesus immediately.

They did not take time to go home and set things in order first. Andrew and Peter did not make sure that someone would come around to take home their nets and tie up their boat. James and John didn't linger on to finish up the labor they had started with their father. All four men heard the call and simply followed.

How much faith must that have taken? A complete stranger showed up and told them to follow him. He may have said more than the Gospel writers recorded, but that isn't important. What matters is that without hesitation the first four disciples knew that they had to follow Jesus, even at great material loss to themselves. Following Jesus isn't easy. As he said himself, it will often involve a lot of sacrifice and suffering.

What if someone came along and told you to leave your job, your family, your possessions, and your wallet behind? How much faith would that take today?

5

꩜

A BACKWARD GLANCE

When the boat had initially been found, Moishele and Yuvi knew in their hearts that it was ancient, but they couldn't identify it as such to anyone else. Their father's pronouncement that the boat was old confirmed this in their minds. But just how old it was, none of them knew.

Kurt and Shelley came to the site and saw the boat, and immediately they identified it as an ancient boat. The mortise and tenon joints used to attach the planks to each other were developed and employed back during the Roman period, almost 2,000 years in the past. The Roman period in Israel, however, lasted hundreds of years. Even after the Jews had been sent into Diaspora (dispersion from their homeland) in 70 A.D., the Romans remained, and so there was a significant window of time from which the boat could have originated.

Not until the preliminary excavation of the boat did the crew get any more specific details about the particular period of time during which the boat would have sailed, full of fish, upon the waters of the Sea of Galilee. The first-century clay oil lamp found in the mud just outside of the boat gave the team a clue about their initial discovery.

As I have said, the lamp could not give conclusive evidence as to the boat's age. First of all, it rested outside of the boat, along with the other pieces of pottery found at the site. The ship had been empty when it finally came to rest, and it is possible the lamp had no connection to the boat whatsoever. In any body of water, the motion of the waves will always be moving things about on the sea or lakebed. The Sea of Galilee experiences some particularly violent sharkias that rush down upon it from the deserts of Syria beyond the Golan Heights and whip up its waters with hardly any warning. These storms are common on the lake, and it was probably a sharkia that Jesus calmed in Matthew 8:23–27. When there are strong winds and waves on the surface, the water beneath is turbulent as well.

You can see evidence of this underwater movement at any beach. Shells wash up on shore after years and years of lying underwater. Pieces of glass, discarded long ago, will come back to beaches showing evidence of their time in the water: Their sharp edges have been rounded by the motion of the waves, grinding them against sand and stones. Water is constantly in motion, and so an oil lamp could have been brought to rest beside a boat that had been there hundreds of years already, or could even be older than the boat beside which it rests.

Understanding that, it is still interesting that the two should be buried side by side. Knowing that wood does not survive long in fresh water, it can be assumed that the silt and mud in which the boat was buried covered it quickly. Since the boat only survived because it was buried in the mud, it may also be assumed that the mud enveloping it kept it pretty well covered. Because the oil lamp had been found beside the boat, there was a reasonable chance that the mud covered up the lamp around the same time as it buried the sunken vessel.

If that was the case, then it seems relatively safe to assume that the boat is from the first century A.D. as well. While the boat's age could be drawn with greater certitude from carbon-14 testing, using the first century as a working date for the excavation shouldn't be too much of a long shot.

If the boat had been in use on the Sea of Galilee in the first century, then it will be helpful to develop a picture of the environment at the time it sailed.

Of course, the first century A.D. in Galilee was the time and place of much of Jesus' life and ministry. As many of his disciples were called from their lives as fishermen, there is some helpful information in the New Testament about the region during this period. However, the Gospel writers were concerned with a subject much different than the social and economic situation of the majority of Galileans at the time.

The Evangelists do not record much in the way of daily life and practices of the people around Christ's native land. Despite the Gospels' silence on these matters, though, there is still a wealth of information about the people and culture of Galilee. Archaeological evidence, longstanding tradition, and records from other sources have provided us with data regarding this period, and so for answers we can turn to the information found in these sources.

Prior to Roman influence entering Israel, the country, along with most of the Middle East, was under the control of the Seleucid Empire. In the first century B.C., the empire was waning quickly, and rival Seleucid factions threatened civil war in Palestine. The Seleucid king in Israel died in 67 B.C. and his two sons began fighting over the throne.

In 63 B.C., before either of the sons could claim the throne, Pompey the Great entered Jerusalem and effectively ended the Seleucid's control. Israel, as part of the Syrian province, was brought under Roman dominion and remained that way past the failure of the Jewish revolt, which occurred between 67–73 A.D. and resulted in the expulsion of many Jews from their homeland. In addition to the exile, many Jews had witnessed a heartbreaking event—the destruction of the Temple in 70 A.D.

In 132, the Jewish leader Bar Kokhba led a revolt against the Romans. After the revolt's initial success, he once again established a Jewish kingdom, of which he was the king. It did not take long for the Romans to send an army to seize the territory from Bar Kokhba, however, and in 135 A.D. Israel was taken away from Jewish hands, seemingly for good.

Under Roman rule, there was for the most part little difference in the everyday lives of the majority of Israelites, as compared with previous circumstances. The majority of the Jews during the period of Roman rule were poor, as were most people at that time. As with most governments at the time, the Romans were harsh and strict but as long as there were no threats of political unrest, provincial governance was left mainly to itself.

While supreme legal jurisdiction resided with the current Roman governor, the Sanhedrin (the Jewish ruling class at the time) was given authority to judge most legal matters for the Jews. The Sanhedrin was not given total authority, however: When Jesus was turned over to Pontius Pilate, it was because the Sanhedrin lacked the power to proclaim a death sentence. Weightier legal matters, such as capital punishment, rested in Roman hands.

Religious matters were left up to the ruling Jewish classes, however. In Jerusalem, worship at the Temple was allowed to continue as long as there was not civil unrest—Roman governors, however, would usually be in town when there were religious holidays and festivals. With large concentrations of religious Jews would gather in Jerusalem for Passover, for instance, the Romans felt as though they should let their physical presence be known. It was important to attempt to discourage any extremists from causing uprisings, although in the case of such uprisings, the governor or ruler never hesitated to use force to bring an immediate halt to the disturbance.

For the most part, however, Roman governance prior to the start of the Great Revolt in 67 A.D. was fairly lenient. Aside from Pontius Pilate, Roman governors respected the sanctity of Jerusalem, and did not force the state religion upon the Jews living there. The Temple sacrifices of Judaism were allowed to continue, and at times were even promoted by the Romans in charge. Herod, in an effort to appease the religious Jews, rebuilt the Temple to the exact specifications of the Temple built by Solomon, and synagogue worship was left unhindered by Roman interference.

This is not to say that Jewish life under Roman occupation was ideal. Many of the Roman rulers such as Herod were arbitrarily cruel to the Israelites, desperate to keep power at any cost. When Herod died in 4 B.C. and his three sons took over the kingdom, the Jews living in Jerusalem sent a delegation to Augustus asking that the rule of Herodians not continue. Their request was denied.

Once in power, Archelaus, one of Herod's sons, was so wicked that a group of Jews once again risked everything to make the journey to Rome and appeal for an audience with Caesar. When their audience was granted, they pleaded with Augustus to remove Archelaus from the throne. Augustus, moved by the Jews' story of suffering, subsequently deposed Archelaus and exiled him to Gaul (Western Europe). In his place, a Roman governor was installed.

Even without an oppressive Roman ruler, life in Israel 2,000 years ago was challenging. Without a strong network of international trade, local agriculture was a necessity, but mostly just the northern parts of the country were cultivated. A small amount of land around Jerusalem was used for crops as well, but not all of the produce was equally distributed. In addition to agriculture, many Israelites raised livestock, but frequently were forced to travel to find pasturelands for their animals.

In Galilee, most of the inhabitants were poor, although the industry practiced there was one of the most important for the region. Most of the land in the region had at one time been royally owned, and so there were few people living there who could afford land-ownership. Much of the time, absentee owners possessed the land and charged fees that made life even harder for those living around the Sea of Galilee. The majority of those living by the lake earned their livelihoods through the fishing industry.

Unfortunately, Galileans were looked down upon by many of their fellow Jews. They spoke a dialect of Aramaic that sounded rough and uneducated to those who were a part of the more Hellenized, Greek-speaking population in cities such as Jerusalem. On top of that, the religious orthodox Jerusalemites, in particular, thought little of their countrymen to the north. Because they were so far from the Temple, strict orthodox Jews suspected that the Galileans did not follow the rules proscribed by Judaism.

On the contrary, these fishermen often tended to be very pious people. Perhaps their piety stemmed from their work environment: When your job is sailing in a small boat in the middle of a lake known for sudden, violent storms, having favor with God takes a prominent position in your life. At least, it seems to have more urgency for people risking their lives than for some of their wealthier countrymen in Jerusalem. There are accounts of shortages of seafood, an important part of everyday diet in areas by large bodies of water, during periods of religious holidays.[1] Fish could not be stored like today, and if fishermen weren't bringing in catches every day, alternative sources of food needed to be utilized.

The poverty experienced by most of the Jews living in Israel was reflected in their homes. Private residences, for the typical family, tended to be small and modest. Remains of houses from this period can be seen at various archaeological sites, but perhaps the most relevant, at least for our discussion, are those found in the ancient town of Capernaum.

At Capernaum, the remnants of family homes have been uncovered and stand waiting for visitors to see. The houses from the first century period were small indeed—often merely a single room for each family, and as often as not at least one wall would be shared with another house. Additionally, these cramped houses would frequently be without a window, so even during the day it would be dark indoors. After a long day's work, the family would settle in for a night's rest, and the entire family would sleep on a single bed.[2]

Private houses, unless the owners were very wealthy, typically could not be locked up. The door could be blocked, possibly with a bolt across the doorway, but because of the close-knit community, it really was not necessary to lock up homes at night. There wasn't much to steal in a house anyway—possessions were few, and a storeroom for grain or tools probably would be equipped with a lock. Other than that, neighbors were free to enter each other's houses at almost any time.

A day in Galilee during the first century A.D. would have been long and tiring. Early in the morning, fishing communities in the towns and villages around the Sea of Galilee were bustling and hard at work. As soon as the sun was up, merchants in the marketplaces were opening their shops and preparing their merchandise for sale.

Women left their homes early to buy the provisions they would need for the day, and the only way to make sure you got everything you needed was to get there first. Water had to be drawn from a well or from the lake, and washing and mending, as well as preparing food for the day, had to be accomplished.

A modern Galilean fisherman
mends his nets

Long before the shops opened, the fishermen had been up tending to their equipment. Nets needed to be checked for holes and tears, and any damage had to be fixed before the nets could be put to use. In order to catch the early morning fish, the fishermen needed to get their gear fixed quickly and get out onto the water before the sun became strong.

For lake and shore workers alike, as much work needed to be finished as possible before the hottest part of the day. In the middle of the day, the communities would wind down and rest indoors or find shelter in the shade because it was unhealthy and unsafe to be exposed. Later in the afternoon, as the heat lessened, everyone went back to get maximum work done before the sun went down.

The boats that sailed upon the waters of the Sea of Galilee were probably fairly uniform—the lack of wealth in the area would not have allowed for many ornate ships, and vessels were constructed with practicality rather than aesthetics in mind. Because of the freshwater bacteria that prove so destructive to wooden crafts, as well as the violent sharkia winds that scream across the lake, the fishing boats were built with the understanding that they would not last terribly long.

Once out on the water, the fishermen used nets to catch fish.

A Galilean casts out his net just as his predecessors did

Hooks may have been used (ancient hooks have been found), but it is more likely that nets were used because they provide a greater yield. Two kinds of nets were put to use: throwing nets and seine nets. Seine nets, or dragnets, vastly bigger than those thrown overboard by hand, were about 500 feet long and reached down a dozen feet. They were dragged through the water either between two boats or between a boat and a fixed point on land. These nets were weighed down on the bottom with anchor stones (Mendel stones) so that they passed through the water like a wall, trapping fish as they were dragged. These nets, being so large, cost quite a bit of money to purchase, and so a lot of work was put in to maintain them. The thrown nets were most common, being less expensive. These nets were simply thrown overboard, with small stones attached to the corners and sides to weigh them down.[3]

When the fishing boats returned to port, the fish were quickly separated according to kind and put into storage tanks. The strict Jewish laws stated which kinds of fish were acceptable to eat, and following the Levitical laws, fish were either thrown back into the lake or kept for sale.

Because the fish had to be kept fresh, on the shore of the Sea of Galilee by the harbors, round stone structures that looked like wells were built. The stones of the tanks were plastered to make them waterproof. These "fish wells" were then filled with the lake's water, and the catches fishermen brought in could be kept alive in the stone tanks until they were brought to the marketplace. Notably, these storage pools used by the fishermen are the same kind of containers mentioned in Matthew 13:48 ("When [the net] was full, men drew it ashore and sat down and sorted the good into containers but threw away the bad").

Because of the high concentration of fish in the area, the harbors must have smelled terrible. Even though most of the fish were kept alive in the artificial pools, a fair amount of fish must have died.

After they were dead, they may have been left in the pools with the other fish, or thrown back into the lake to wash against the shore. Perhaps they were even thrown on the ground. When the sun was at its full strength, the fishermen could all seek shelter in the shade, but the fish were left stranded in their crowded tanks. As the sun beat down upon the fish pools, the growing stench must have been unbearable.

Because the fishermen as individuals were quite poor, they frequently banded together in groups. This practice was helpful both for the actual act of fishing and when it came time to go to market with their catches. Pooling their resources, the fishermen could buy equipment that they could never have afforded by themselves. When they had to sell their fish at the market, their status as a group gave them additional leverage, much like unions today. Merchants and vendors, who otherwise would pay the fishermen as little as possible, found themselves pressured to provide fair prices for the fish.

In the New Testament (Luke 5:1–11), three of the soon-to-be disciples were fishing on the Sea of Galilee when Christ appeared and told them to cast their nets into the water. Though Simon Peter was doubtful they would find anything, he obeyed, and they landed a miraculous catch so big they had to call in their other boat. There is no mention of Simon Peter, James, or John being wealthy, so it is likely that the other boat they had to call over to help carry the load was crewed by members of a "fishing union" to which the three disciples belonged.

People around the Sea of Galilee relied on their neighbors and friends for support. These "fishing unions" were a result of the close social bonds shared between people in a given community. Everything about the lifestyles of Galileans points to this close bond: the small, single-room houses ensured a close-knit family; fishermen kept in close association and banded together for support and assistance.

True, most of the leisure-time activities were practiced by the upper class—the Romans especially—but Jewish children in poor, rural areas still had games to play. Balls were in use, though not rubber balls, as we know today. Of course it goes without saying that children in ancient Israel did not throw around the old pigskin, but nonetheless, ball games had been invented by then. It is impossible at this point to know how the games were played and what the rules may have been, but at the end of the day children were surely running around, playing in the fields outside the towns and villages with their friends.

For a fishing community built on the shores of the Sea of Galilee, life depended upon the waters of the lake. While not every fisherman could own a boat, each likely had a share in one. Unfortunately, the fresh water of the Sea of Galilee was destructive to wood. The bacteria living in the warm water would, over the years a boat was in use, eat away at the planking, before long making the craft unfit for carrying heavy cargos of fish.

Because a boat was such an investment for these fishermen, they would have stretched each one as far as they could. Even as a group, fishermen probably could not afford to have a new boat constructed every ten or fifteen years—in addition to the cost of hiring a shipwright (a ship builder), lumber was difficult to come by. There were trees around, for sure, but not every kind of wood was ideal for use in shipbuilding. To preserve their fishing boats, pitch was smeared on the outside of the planking. This kept the wood intact longer than it naturally would have lasted, but even that wore off after a while.

In the event of a sharkia, some boats must have inevitably been destroyed. While a tragedy for the boat's owners and crew, scrambles took place after each major storm to scour the beach for pieces of wood broken off wrecked boats. These planks, along with other hard-to-come-by pieces of wood, were used to keep fishing boats repaired. As long as the majority of the wood was still sound, broken or rotted planks could be replaced, and boats were made to last past their normal lifespan.

Galilee in the first century A.D. was a hard place to live, but the people who lived there knew how to get by, and had generations of training and wisdom to support them. A boat such as the one found by Yuvi and Moishele was the world to most Galileans of that time period. Fishing built the region, and without it, ancient Galilee would have been a drastically different place.

However, prior to further investigation, the boat could only be assumed to be from the first century. The auxiliary discoveries in the mud next to the boat provided hints at the boat's original time period, but nothing could be conclusively proven, yet. Proof of the boat's age would have to wait until samples of its timbers could be analyzed with carbon-14 testing.

6

❧

Build Me a Boat

Once the boat had been removed from the excavation site, it was time to start thinking about learning more details from its past. There had been a few artifacts found around the site—the oil lamp had been the first, but a cooking pot and other potsherds had turned up as well. All of these auxiliary artifacts dated the boat roughly to the first century A.D. At least, that's what they seemed to date back to at first glance. With a little down time at hand, it was time the artifacts should be taken to experts to have more exact dates ascribed to them.

Seventeen[1] distinct pieces of ancient pottery had been discovered at the site. Most of these pieces were only fragments, but the oil lamp and a cooking pot that had been found were complete pieces. It is important to note once again that these pieces of ancient pottery, while found in the immediate vicinity of the boat, were not the ship's cargo. The boat had been found pretty much empty, and the other artifacts that turned up were impossible to connect with the boat. The motion of the water in the lake could easily have brought them to rest near the boat, or if the location had been in the distant past a ship graveyard, it is certainly possible that other things would have been cast away in the same location.

Evidence given by the fragments themselves indicates, however, that for the most part the potsherds did not spend significant periods of time being swept over the lakebed by the water. In fact, only one piece out of the collection of seventeen collected from the excavation site showed signs of "water wear," or smooth, weathered edges caused by prolonged motion in water.[2] What does this mean?

Simply, it tells us something quite similar to what the boat tells us. It has already been established that freshwater allows certain wood-eating bacteria to breed, and had the boat been exposed for a long period of time, it would have been destroyed. The very fact of the boat's survival shows that the rate of sedimentation was very high—silt and mud covered the site rapidly after the boat had been sunk. The fact that sixteen of seventeen pieces of pottery were not worn down by the effects of the Sea of Galilee's water is another sign that the mud accumulated quickly, enveloping the pieces of pottery before their broken edges could be smoothed over by the water.

The fragments discovered within a relatively small distance of the boat represent a variety of pottery types. The collection includes eight pieces from cooking pots (one complete pot and seven fragments), five fragments from storage pots, the oil lamp, and sherds from jugs. The assortment of different types of pottery would seem to indicate that this area was highly trafficked and most likely residential. The site of the boat was at least part of or adjacent to a port or market, with a fair amount of people passing by it.

Nearly all of the pieces of pottery could be dated (there were two fragments that weren't dateable[3]), and so provide a good clue into the approximate time at which the sediment built up and covered the fragments. The styles of the pottery fragments are what can be dated—carbon-14 dating doesn't work on materials like clay as it does with wood. Because the dates provided by design style are not exact, examining the pottery gives a historical range rather than a precise time period.

Pottery styles are relatively easy to use for dating purposes, as long as the person giving the date estimates knows what she is doing. In a region like Galilee, there was a lot of trade, so pottery styles were continually being adapted and modified to reflect the fashion "in vogue" at the time. On top of that, if the person studying the artifacts is well informed as to the history of the location, even more information can be gathered.

In the region around the Sea of Galilee, history plays a crucial role in determining what archaeological discoveries can tell experts. Looking at the pottery, it can be seen that the design styles that came about toward the end of the first century A.D. are noticeably absent from the site. Subtle variations such as the shape of the handles or mouths of jars have been identified at other excavation sites relatively near to the shore where the boat was found. Particularly because other excavations take place in a much more controlled environment, dates can be drawn easily from the variety of artifacts discovered. Comparing styles of pottery fragments found at other sites with the fragments found around the boat can provide additional details about when such styles were in use.

Using these techniques, a date range for the pottery was established. This range, at first glance, is fairly large. It encompasses a period from the mid first-century B.C. through the mid second-century A.D. That range presents a period of roughly 200 years from which the pottery could have originated. Some detective work will carry us a little bit farther in understanding when these fragments were in use.

This is where history comes into play. Remember that some of the subtle variations in pottery styles typical of the region were not displayed in the fragments that were recovered by the boat. Basically, the pottery reflects no change in style past the mid to late first-century A.D., the later, rather generous dates given above being an attempt to indicate how long after they fell out of style the old pots and jugs may still have been in use. Now try to remember if anything happened around the area where the boat was found that could explain the lack of newer pottery styles.

In the late first century A.D., some of the Jews living around the Sea of Galilee revolted against the Roman occupation. The Battle of Migdal took place in 67 A.D., two-thirds of the way through the century. The Roman forces obliterated the Jewish rebels that had presented resistance to their rule, drastically altering the social setting for the years to come.

Although many of the people who were either killed or sold into slavery by the Romans were determined to have come from outside Migdal[4], there were still many native Migdalites who were caught up in the massacre. The Roman cavalry that entered the ancient city likely didn't scrutinize their victims too carefully. They had entered a hostile city and were trying to cause as much damage as possible in order to break the fighters' spirits. When the bloodbath was finished, a significant portion of Migdal's population had probably been slain.

The drastic impact that this loss of life would have had on ancient society is reflected in the pottery that turned up at the excavation site. The city most likely did not recover for quite some time, and many of its citizens may have chosen to leave because of the horrors they now associated with their homes. For whatever reason, it is likely because of the Battle of Migdal that the area is devoid of pottery after a certain period.

That gives us an end date of roughly 70 A.D. for the pottery fragments (this same reasoning can help provide an end point for the boat's date range as well), narrowing the range down to about 100 years. It would still be helpful if it were possible to narrow down the range a bit more.

If the origin date of the style of the pottery fragments discovered at the site can be fixed at the mid first-century B.C., that doesn't mean that those vessels were created right away. Since our understanding is that the same style was in use during the whole time period, the clay pots these fragments originated from could have been made at the turn of the century, or even later. On top of that is the fact that new pots and lamps would not have been purchased simply because there was a new, more "in" style being made. The social situation was such that most of the people around the Sea of Galilee would not have been in the position to afford luxury items—they bought what they needed, and you can be sure they got as much mileage out of each item as they could.

The dating is most specific with the oil lamp. Certain features that it displays, such as the shape of the handle and the red clay, tools, and techniques used in its construction, place it in the Herodian period[5], the period during which Christ lived. Using these criteria, the pottery provides a date range only a few decades larger either way than the time of Christ's life in Israel.

Of course, the date of the boat cannot be conclusively given by scattered fragments of broken pottery. The manner in which they were strewn about the site provides only an ambiguous, possibly entirely coincidental, connection to the ancient boat. In order to actually get a date for the boat, a more precise method of dating needed to be employed. Thankfully, the perfect form of dating was available to the archaeologists working on the boat: carbon-14, or radiocarbon dating.

It is important to establish exactly what carbon-14 dating means before going into results. At the most basic level, all living things on Earth have carbon in them—thus the phrase carbon-based life forms. When one of those living things dies, whether it is a whale, a human, or a tree, it ceases to produce carbon. It is to that point that a carbon-14 analysis will date, not when it first began living.

Specifically, what is measured in this process is a particular isotope of carbon, C-14 (the test is referred to by the isotope it measures). Simply put, an isotope is an atom that has a different number of protons than usual. This isotope is radioactive, or rather it is unstable. That doesn't mean that exposure to C-14 will cause harm to a person; it only means that over time the isotope will degrade.

All radioactive isotopes have what is called a half-life. The half-life of an isotope is measured in years and indicates how many years it takes for half of the isotope to degrade. For example, let's say I have 100 grams of a radioactive material with a half-life of 50 years. Fifty years from now I will have 50 grams; 100 years from now I will have 25 grams; and so on.

Carbon-14 dating tests how much of the isotope is left in the sample. This particular isotope has a half-life of 5,570 years, and so the calculations are based off of that. Because the test works with large numbers, there is also an amount of variance built into each result, similar to the margin of error given with poll results. This means that the further back you can date, the more accurate the test will be. If something is dated to be 100 years old, the margin of error could give it an age anywhere from 180 to 20 years old. A result that comes back saying an artifact is 50,000 years old is therefore extremely precise—a few decades of difference is fairly negligible at that point.

———

When samples of the boat were sent out, Kurt and Shelley wanted to make sure that the results were as unbiased as possible. There was so much media attention surrounding the excavation that they needed to ensure the results they received were accurate in order to stand up to the scrutiny that would surely follow. With that in mind, ten samples were taken from the boat and sent to three separate laboratories around the world. They made sure not to inform the technicians where the wood samples had come from; they just needed the dates without any speculation.

When the results from the independent tests were returned, they all gave the same information. Each laboratory had determined the average ages of the wood samples to be 40 B.C., with a margin of error of 80 years. These results meant that the trees used to make the lumber for the boat had been chopped down at the date provided—the point at which C-14 was no longer being produced.

The carbon-14 tests had yielded a date range for the boat's wood of 120 B.C. to 40 A.D. Sometime in that period of 160 years, the trees the boat was made of had ceased to live. After they had been chopped down, it would have taken some time for the wood to dry and be converted into planks. Seeing as the modern lumberyard and sawmill were not in use during that period, it is probably fair to assume that the process would have taken a considerable time to complete.

It will also be beneficial to stop here and think about the conclusions that Richard Steffy drew from his time studying the boat. Admittedly, he thought little of its craftsmanship when he first saw it. He was disappointed, and thought it a "shoddily-built craft, a far cry from the structural finesse found on Mediterranean hulls of the Classical period, and one which had been repaired and patched frequently by an amateur."[6] However, before much of the time for his short trip to Israel had gone by, he had changed his mind about the boat.

It had seemed at first that the ancient boat builder hadn't possessed a good knack for choosing his materials. The wood utilized in the boat's construction had come from twelve different kinds of trees, not all of which provided typical or appropriate material for shipbuilding. Some of the woods were usually considered too soft for the durability needed for a long life on the water; some were only used once, as though the original builder had been unable to distinguish between the new wood and his usual material.

It is amazing that there should be twelve different woods used in the construction of this boat. It would seem much more likely that a craft such as this would have been built with the use of years of experience. If boats had been in use for centuries on the Sea of Galilee, it is probable that each new generation of shipwrights learned what materials were the best for new construction. Assuming that to be the case, it would make sense that there was one type of wood generally understood to be optimal for hull construction, possibly another type for frames and support, and maybe another for oars and a mast. For there to be twelve different types of wood in the boat appears very unusual.

What Steffy quickly saw as he inspected the boat more carefully was that the boatwright had known exactly what he was doing. In a report he wrote on the book, he states that there were two likely reasons for the boat being constructed of such poor quality wood: One, the availability of proper wood was limited in the region at the time; or two, the person who had hired the builder to construct a boat had set a small, tight budget for the project.[7] Steffy's conclusion is that the first option is much more likely than the second.

A close inspection of the boat's timbers allowed for the realization that much of the wood had been used on the boat secondhand. Most likely because it was too difficult to buy new, fresh-cut wood,

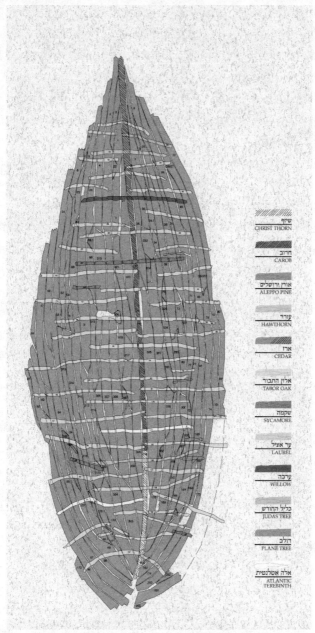

שיזף
CHRIST THORN

חרוב
CAROB

אורן ירושלים
ALEPPO PINE

עוזרר
HAWTHORN

ארז
CEDAR

אלון התבור
TABOR OAK

שקמה
SYCAMORE

ער אציל
LAUREL

ערבה
WILLOW

כליל החורש
JUDAS TREE

דולב
PLANE TREE

אלה אטלנטית
ATLANTIC
TEREBINTH

The twelve different woods that make up this ancient boat

a large part of this boat had been built using recycled materials. Evidence of this fact was soon apparent as Steffy looked at the individual planks. The strings that Danny had affixed to the boat had revealed unusually thin planks in many places. Whereas those planks had initially been thought to be evidence of an inferior carpenter, it soon became clear that it had been a master carpenter working with inferior materials.

The planks looked narrow because they were fragments that had to have been built up into a normal-sized plank. In order to do so, the ancient craftsman needed to cut down each plank to remove the grooves cut for mortise and tenon joints. By the time each piece of wood was smooth and sound, it was much smaller than a typical boat's plank ought to have been. The individual small planks then had to be joined together to make up a new, properly sized plank to be fit onto the ship's frame. These composite planks convinced Steffy that the builder had been fully trained and was much more skilled than he originally thought. He acknowledged, after scrutiny of his work, that the boat's builder had had a "well founded [discipline] that was capable of producing a strong and practical boat in spite of the lack of good compass timber."[8]

In addition to the thriftiness displayed in the original construction of the boat, numerous repairs were evident as Steffy reviewed the hull's structure. It seemed the life of the boat had been prolonged due to these repairs. It was apparent, due to the differences of the tool marks, that there had been multiple craftsmen who had worked on the boat over the period of its life on the Sea of Galilee.

The harsh bacterial conditions fostered by the Sea of Galilee's fresh water, in addition to the frequent storms, had taken their toll. Much of the wood faced deterioration and needed to be replaced. Because of the apparent scarcity of wood, building a new boat seemed likely to be out of the question. The best option remaining was to use whatever lumber was available to patch up the leaky hull to get some extra mileage out of it.

Because the boat had obviously been repaired numerous times, the length of time it had been in service is difficult to determine. Regardless, this information gives us two more factors that can help provide a better idea of the date range in which the boat sailed the Sea of Galilee. In addition to the extended life the boat enjoyed due to its repairs, the fact that a majority of its hull was constructed using recycled timbers pushes back the carbon-14 dates a bit more. The oldest timbers on the boat, the ones that had been dated the furthest back, could easily have been recycled from a previous ship. If that was the case, then they might have seen a decade of use or more on their first vessel, and the boat that Yuvi and Moishele found might not have been built until many years after the oldest trees had first been cut down.

Eventually, the hull reached a point of deterioration where it was no longer worth repairing. Just as it had been built using pieces from old boats, this boat had been brought to shore and planks in good condition were salvaged, probably for use in other boats. Many pieces were missing from the boat when it was uncovered from the mud, but not all of them had rotted away. The upper planks had—because they had not been buried by sediment, the bacteria in the freshwater had completely destroyed them. Sections of the boat had, it seemed, been purposely removed.

Steffy and the other archaeologists were able to tell that certain timbers had been carefully removed, rather than ripped off, because the sections from which they had been taken were not damaged at all. All signs pointed to a scenario that had the boat being brought up on shore and scavenged. There were no top decks or a mast found anywhere on the site—that valuable wood had been removed before the hull was abandoned. The boat almost certainly wasn't destroyed in a storm (besides, it was right up by the beach). Because it had been repaired so much, and with such inferior materials, it is fairly certain that the owner(s) of this boat were not wealthy. They needed to keep their boat floating as long as they could, because as much as high-quality repairs were out of the question, they could even less afford to buy a new boat.

A merchant would probably not be a poor boat-owner, so unless a miserly businessman had wanted to pinch pennies, it's almost certain that this boat had been a fishing boat. If you remember, there were often groups of fishermen who formed alliances, ancient fishing "unions." There is a possibility that one such union of fishermen had owned this boat, and the repairs indicate their lack of disposable income.

There are also other indicators that point to our ancient craft being a fishing boat.

Aside from the fact that this is the first and only ancient boat to be found in the Sea of Galilee, not many depictions of watercraft exist from the biblical period. Thus, it is difficult to know both what the boat looked like and what it was used for.

On the other hand, maritime history on Israel's Mediterranean coast has been extremely well documented. Because of the preserving properties of salt water, complete ships have been found in that sea. Being able to look at whole wrecks is a boon for archaeologists, but it also made the Galilee boat that much more frustrating—while the hull was intact, the upper portions of the planking, the decks, and the mast were all gone (although much of that is probably a result of salvaging). As frustrating as our boat's state of preservation was at times for the archaeologists, the fact remains that it was vastly more than had ever been found before. In addition to that, the intact hull gives a good idea of how the Galilee boat compares with the ships built and used in the Mediterranean.

Based on the ships he had studied previously, as he looked over the boat at Ginosar, Steffy was able to draw some conclusions. In Shelley Wachsmann's book, he explains how Professor Steffy had, on his first full day at the site, drawn some sketches of what he believed the boat's complete and intact hull would have looked like when it was in use.[9]

According to Steffy's appraisal of the hull, the boat would have been crewed by four oarsmen when the wind was low. On top of that, it almost certainly was equipped with a large sail to take advantage of favorable winds. The length and width of the hull also give a clue as to how many people could have fit inside the boat. With its size, it probably could have held between twelve and fifteen men at a time.

Soon after Steffy had shown Shelley his rough sketches, two men dropped by the excavation site. When I met with Kurt, he told me that clergymen had been to visit the boat during its excavation. Those clergymen apparently were Franciscans with a penchant for archaeology—they had participated in digs in Capernaum and Migdal, and were interested in seeing this new discovery. With how many people showed up to assist the excavation, it seems that almost every other person in Israel has a bent toward archaeology.

One of these Franciscan friars approached Shelley and talked with him about the boat. Because of his own personal interest in archaeology, he wanted to know about this discovery. After all, this boat, like many other discoveries in Israel, had the potential to cross the boundary between his hobby and his calling. Once Shelley had explained what they knew about the boat so far, Father Corbo revealed that he had not come to visit the site empty-handed.

It wasn't that the Franciscans had brought anything material with them, but Father Corbo shared a piece of information with Shelley that would prove most useful. In the course of their archaeological pursuits, the two clergymen had been part of an excavation that uncovered a first-century home in Migdal. Laid into the floor of the house was a mosaic that had since been removed and taken to the Franciscan monastery. One corner of that mosaic was filled with a picture of a boat.

When Shelley heard this, his eyes lit up. Could it be possible? Was this mosaic from the same time period as the boat still partially buried just a stone's throw behind him? He had to see what the boat in the mosaic looked like.

There wasn't time to run over to Migdal now to look at the mosaic—it would be better if he went once the excavation was completed. Since he felt he needed to see the mosaic, though, he handed a notebook to Father Corbo and asked if he would mind sketching the boat in the mosaic. The friar willingly took Shelley's pen.

In the notebook, he drew out a rough outline of a ship and then handed the drawing to Shelley. Its shape, notwithstanding the addition of a mast and sail, was the spitting image of the sketch Steffy had drawn a short while earlier. When Shelley asked Father Corbo if the picture in the mosaic included any oars, he took back the sketch and quickly indicated three of them alongside the hull. Shelley thanked him and rushed to show the image to Steffy.[10]

The good news about this latest discovery was that there was an ancient illustration of a boat fairly contemporary with the craft currently under excavation. The mosaic presented the excavators with a good idea of what their boat may have looked like, or at least what other boats on the Sea of Galilee at the time were like. This was the first visual depiction of watercraft from the same time and place as the boat. The bad news, however, was that this was probably not a visual depiction of the specific kind of boat they were excavating. If the boat in the mosaic had three oars on a side, it meant the boat in the picture was larger than the boat buried in the mud. Steffy had

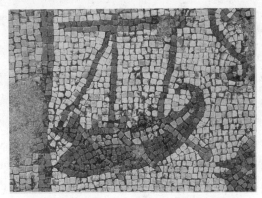

The ancient mosaic discovered at Migdal

been pretty sure that the ancient boat at the dig would not have had more than two oars to a side.

His original enthusiasm about the mosaic dampened, Shelley still wanted to take some time and properly look into it. It might be the case that it didn't depict a replica of the boat he was seeing rescued from the mud, but it was still more to go on than they had previously had. It would be a waste if he didn't investigate the mosaic a bit more thoroughly, but that scrutiny would need to wait a short while. The actual excavation had to come first.

When the boat's excavation phase was completed, Shelley finally had the time he needed to check out the mosaic. Danny had taken a few shots of it while the excavation was still ongoing, and Shelley had converted those shots to slides. To better familiarize himself with the mosaic, Shelley set up a projector and a clean sheet of paper and began to trace the picture of ancient mosaic onto a personal copy. As he finished up his picture, he was struck with amazement. The final oar he drew, the last oar toward the back of the boat, was not an oar after all! As he traced its outline onto his paper, Shelley realized that the business end of the "oar," the part that dips into the water, was too wide. The other two oars in the picture fit, but their blades were only one stone wide—at the blade the final oar was two stones wide.

It only took a moment of puzzled, head-scratching thought for Shelley to come up with the solution to the mind-teaser: There were only two oars on the boat in the mosaic. The third "oar" was actually a rudder![11] If that was indeed the case, then the boat in the mosaic was the same design and style as Steffy had predicted with his sketch during the excavation. It seemed he had been right, and that the boat would have had two oars to a side. The boat in the mosaic was, after all, a contemporary of the boat Yuvi and Moishele had found by the shores of the Sea of Galilee!

This realization was a huge windfall for study surrounding the boat. Prior to Shelley figuring out how well the Migdal boat mosaic correlated to the boat he had helped excavate, nobody could really be certain what the boat had looked like, what its purposes could have been, and how many people it could have held. With the boat in the mosaic at last identified as the same type as the boat found at Ginosar, the archaeologists begin to draw some conclusions about their discovery.

The ship most likely looked very much like the boat in the mosaic. As with generations of shipwrights deciding which type of timber would be best for boat construction, there was probably a general model for boats in the Sea of Galilee. They had to be built with sharkias in mind, but the lake does not have strong currents like a river does, and a ship's hull would not need to withstand the daily pounding of waves that boats in the Mediterranean Sea were up against. Most, if not all of the boats on the Sea of Galilee during the first century A.D. would have looked rather similar.

So the boat the Lufan brothers discovered would have required a crew of five men on board—enough to steer the boat and man the four oars at need. The mosaic, pulled from the first-century A.D. home in Migdal, was of the same type as the ancient boat. Remember that Steffy's sketch was not based on the mosaic—he predicted the boat's shape from the hull while it sat in the mud. Because there was no influence from one artifact to the other, it's more than just a good chance that the hull pulled from the mud matches the image in the mosaic.

Based on all the available dating methods, the boat certainly seemed to be from around the first century A.D. Carbon dating, the pottery, even the mosaic—they all provided the archaeologists with roughly the same date for the boat. There was still a lot left to do to take care of the boat, however, and if the boat made it through conservation, the future would bring more tests and more answers.

7

ℑ

A Bath for a Boat

Although the excavation of the boat was complete, there was still a vast amount of work to complete before the boat was truly "saved." The excavation was really only the first stage of rescuing the boat—eleven days was a short period for an archaeological dig, and those eleven days made up only a miniscule fraction (less than a quarter of a percent) of the time it would take to conserve the boat.

Two considerations in rescuing the boat were notably different. In the excavation process, the boat had to be removed with care from the environment that had protected it for hundreds of years. During that time, it had become extremely fragile, and any excessive pressure placed upon its timbers would likely pull the whole thing apart. While carrying out the excavation, everyone on the site was in a tricky position—the boat was rapidly drying out, so the dig needed to be finished as soon as possible. On the flip side of that, haste often makes waste and if speed took priority over caution, the boat could easily have been destroyed.

Once the boat had spent the night floating in the harbor at Ginosar, it turned the corner in its new life as an artifact—it was time to begin the conservation.

On the first day after the completion of the excavation, the crew's mindset had to undergo a radical change. The outcome of the dig had been the removal of a weak relic from the natural environment that had protected it for nearly 2,000 years. Even though that removal was necessary for the boat's ultimate survival, it was still a detrimental action for the boat. Out of the mud, it might begin to rapidly deteriorate. Orna's job as conservator was to make sure that the boat could survive in a new environment: on display in a museum. She needed a lot of help to get the boat to that point.

Orna had already determined how to preserve the boat—full immersion in a bath of PEG (polyethylene glycol). The cocooning of the vessel whole in polyurethane foam had, after all, been done for that reason. There was only one thing that stood between the boat and its preservation: There was no sufficiently sized pool on hand to soak the boat in.

Thankfully, the solution was once again provided for the boat. Because construction was wrapping up but still ongoing at the Yigal Allon Museum, a construction crew was already on site and could build a tank for the boat. The location for the tank was decided upon, and a crane was brought alongside the beach.

While that was happening, Shelley took someone down to Ginosar's harbor and tied a towline between the ancient boat and a motorboat. The motorboat was used to bring the polyurethane-encased boat back up the lake to the museum, but it took a long time. Still trying to be careful not to jostle the boat, the motorboat had to be driven slow enough so that there wouldn't be a wake. It probably wasn't much faster than if the two men had simply tied the ropes around their waists and swum the boat to the museum themselves.

While the boat was in transit, a makeshift platform was constructed and fixed to the end of the crane. When the boat drew up alongside the beach upon which the preservation tank would be built, the crane operator lowered the platform into the Sea of Galilee, just in front of the boat. Hearts pounding in their chests, the onlookers watched as the boat was floated on top of the platform and slowly began to rise from the water.

Water dripped off of the boat as it hung suspended in the air, floating over everyone's heads. The crane had to move the boat slowly and carefully to the beach, which was still muddy—if the crane slipped or lost balance, it would jolt the cable. If that happened . . . no one was willing to entertain that notion.

Still, though, as the boat hung in front of their eyes, the question hung right in the back of everyone's minds: What if? How recently had the cable been checked to see if it was in good condition? How firmly planted was the crane? How securely had the platform been attached to the cable? Their hopes and dreams were literally hanging by a thread: a thick, braided steel thread, anyway.

Preparations are made to lift the boat out of the water

*Volunteers watch as the boat is lifted out of the water
and over their heads*

The worry was understandable. So many problems had cropped up during the excavation. It was almost uncanny that nothing should go wrong during this step—setbacks and obstacles had been the hallmark of the dig. Thankfully, at this point, one of the most delicate moments of the boat's rescue, nothing went wrong. Despite any sudden apprehension anyone might have developed, the cable held and the boat was delicately laid down upon the beach. Next to the boat, a large, white rectangular box had been drawn in the mud—the site of the conservation tank.

Now that the boat had safely arrived at the conservation site, precise measurements could be taken. The white lines drawn on the ground only represented a rough guess as to how large the tank would need to be. While still at the excavation site, the workers had been unable to properly measure the boat, and so the exact dimensions of the tank couldn't be determined.

Isaac Rotem, the contractor for the Yigal Allon Museum, became the coordinator for the construction of the boat's conservation tank. While taking the boat's measurements for the tank's dimensions, he had to strike a delicate balance. The entire project was on an extremely tight budget, and it would take a huge amount of PEG to fill the tank so that the boat would be fully immersed.

At this point, Orna wasn't sure where they could obtain such a large amount of the chemical, so Rotem's task was to make the tank as small as possible. The volume of the pool had to be sufficiently large to hold the boat, but not much more. The greater its volume, the more PEG would have to be used, driving up the cost of the conservation. Its interior dimensions were finally set so both the boat and workers would fit in the container.

It took ten days for the boat's pool to be constructed, and Rotem made sure that it met all of Orna's specifications. The walls of the pool were insulated with 5 centimeters of Styrofoam and then lined with glossy white ceramic tiles. Orna needed to make sure as little energy escaped from the tank as possible. The preservation of the boat would take years, and the synthetic PEG wax needed to be kept around 60° Celsius (140° Fahrenheit). Seeing as the electricity required to keep the temperature constant would be yet another expense, Orna wanted to make sure that the tank would retain as much of that heat as it could.

Once the tank had been completed, it was time to move the boat once more. The tank could not have been constructed around the boat—there was too much of a risk that something could fall on it and cause it to break. Needing to lift it from the mud into the pool, one of the team members arranged for a crane to come and hoist the boat into its temporary home.

When the crane arrived, it was parked next to the tank and preparations were made to lift the boat once again. The operator jumped out of the truck and began fixing the huge machine where it sat, placing boards underneath its extendable hydraulic legs. If you remember, the beach had been deemed unsuitable for a heavy truck to drive the boat from the excavation site to the preservation site—it was loose, and there was a likelihood of getting stuck. The crane operator wanted to make sure that his crane would be securely planted on this unstable surface, particularly since the package he was about to lift was irreplaceable.

Once the crane had been stabilized, its cable was affixed to the lifting platform upon which the boat rested and the boat once more took flight. The excavators felt apprehensive, but having seen the boat successfully moved by crane ten days earlier, they had developed some trust in the equipment.

The boat was gently raised above everyone's heads, and delicately swung directly above the preservation tank. Some men had wisely climbed atop the walls of the pool to help guide the boat into place—there was not a lot of extra space, so the boat had to be lowered precisely to avoid it banging into the walls. It turned out that fitting the boat into the tank was more difficult than originally thought.

While the crane's operator was trying to angle the polyurethane package into just the right position, the unthinkable happened. Under the stress of the weight of the boat, one of the crane's hydraulic legs shifted and slipped off of the plank that had supported it. Suddenly destabilized, the crane jolted, jerking the cable and the boat along with it. The crane operator lost control of the crane's arm and the boat's momentum swung it into the side of the preservation tank.[1]

Thinking quickly, he drove the loose hydraulic leg deep into the mud, stabilizing the crane again, but too late. The trust that everyone had placed in him had been violated—that sudden jolt might even have broken up the boat within its foam cocoon. With this boat, there were no second chances. The crane operator was dismissed from the site.

The following day, another crane with another operator arrived at the site. The group was wary to put the boat at the mercy of another crane, but they really had no choice. Thankfully, the spot that this crane parked in was more level and more conducive to maintaining stability. This time, without any mishaps, the boat at last found its way into the preservation tank.

Now it was time for yet another difficult task. The polyurethane foam that had protected the boat for two weeks had to be removed from its hull in order to preserve the wood. This, as with everything else in the project, proved easier said than done.

The excavators initially thought the polyurethane could be removed simply with hot tools. Foam tends not to hold up under heat, so an electrically heated knife would pass through the polyurethane almost as easily as it would pass through butter. This way, saws would not have to be employed to cut away the foam, thus posing a threat to the wood underneath if the sawing was not stopped in time.

Unfortunately, there is a particular property of polyurethane that had been overlooked. When heated (such as when cut with a heated knife) a chemical reaction occurs, producing cyanide gas. In

Placing the boat inside the preservation tank

the confined quarters of the conservation pool, it would be far too hazardous to create this cyanide gas. As precious as this boat was, the lives of the people working on it were a higher priority, and the easy and expedient "hot knife" method was abandoned.

This left one option, which was by no means easy or expedient. The boat would have to be excavated once again, this time from polyurethane. Unsure how the boat was holding up inside its foam cover, excavation of the hull began immediately and was sustained at a frustrating snail's pace. First, openings were cut along the sides of the boat at the top to allow water to be dripped down onto the ancient wood. A drainage hole was likewise cut at the bottom of the package, so that the entire thing didn't fill up with water.

At first, the polyurethane could be cut off in large segments from the boat without fear of harming the actual timbers. Before long, yellowish chunks of foam began filling up the pool, stripped from the craft. Volunteers collected and removed the pieces of foam that collected on the bottom of the tank to keep it clear for the excavators.

As the digging got closer to the wood, it became more difficult

Excavators begin "re-excavating" the boat

to remove the polyurethane. It had to be chipped off, but not at the expense of the boat. While the foam was being painstakingly taken off of the sides and interior of the vessel, Danny, the photographer, was digging tunnels underneath the boat, much the same way he had done in the mud. Limited by the narrow confines of the tank, Danny was the only person left who was small enough to squeeze under the boat for the time-consuming operation.

While he dug each tunnel through the polyurethane, David created new supports for the boat out of fiberglass and PVC piping. Every time a tunnel was finished, a support leg was placed on each side of the boat's hull to make sure the craft didn't fall over or snap in half.[2]

The heavy fumes created by the resin used to harden the fiberglass filled the pool, making the conditions even harder to work in. Even though the tank was open at the top, the cramped, tight space retained the stench. Because of this, the long days spent in the preservation pool seemed even longer.

Another difficulty in re-excavating the boat was that many of the volunteer workers had left Ginosar. The excitement of the initial excavation had faded, and after the boat had been "sailed" to the museum, many people felt as though they would no longer be needed. After all, some of them had spent nearly two weeks working on the project and needed to get back to their normal jobs and responsibilities.

In a way, it was good that many people had left. This time around, there wasn't room in the pool and the tank for nearly as many people, and had all the volunteers stayed on for this second phase, quite a few of them would have had nothing to do. Had there been more workers available, however, shorter shifts might have made the task a bit easier on the re-excavators. There might even have been other people small enough to join Danny in digging the tunnels beneath the boat.

As it was, there remained only the dedicated few who stuck it out until all the necessary work was done. They were focused and determined to get the job finished, and they worked all day to accomplish that as quickly as they could. Still, fewer workers meant the job would take longer, which was turning into more of a problem than anyone had thought.

The way Orna and Rotem had designed the tank proved to be brilliant. The insulation built into it really worked—unfortunately it was more detrimental to the boat's rescue than it was helpful at this stage. The insulation had been installed to keep the temperature of the PEG high once it had been pumped into the pool. High temperatures wouldn't be a problem once the boat was submerged, but as the polyurethane was scraped off and the wood was exposed once again, the insulation trapped the sun's heat inside the pool. Every day that the wood was exposed to the sun and the heat, it was drying out.

Try as they might, the excavators could not keep the boat hydrated. Some of the volunteers were continually employed spraying the hull with water, but theirs was a losing battle. The heat from the

Cutting the foam off of the boat was a painstaking process

sun was more powerful than the perpetual misting could fight, and as it beat down sections of the wood became visibly dry.

That was bad. The excavators hadn't been fooling themselves: They all knew that spraying the wood wasn't any sort of permanent remedy. The only way to keep the boat waterlogged was to keep it underwater. That option was tantalizingly available to the crew the entire time the boat was being freed from the polyurethane. Once they were done chipping all the insulating foam from the ancient vessel, the tank in which it sat would be flooded with water. Why not just fudge it a little and fill it up a bit early?

Aside from the fact that all the wood needed to be exposed for the preservation process (even the fiberglass support ribs were being cut thinner to present as much of the wood to the PEG as was possible), if the pool were flooded with water now, the ship would be under an enormous level of stress. The exposed wood had very different buoyancy than the polyurethane foam.

When the boat needed to be transported, it was easy to "sail" it, because the polyurethane it was covered with floats. On its own, however, it was just a mass of waterlogged wood, which left by itself in water will sink. If an attempt were made to submerge the boat now, the boat itself would try to stay on the bottom of the pool while the lighter polyurethane foam would be fighting to lift the boat to the water's surface. With the structural integrity of packing peanuts, the ancient wood simply could not withstand such forces pulling at it. The ship would almost certainly break apart if they tried to submerge it now, only partially freed from the polyurethane.

Every day that went by without the foam being totally removed meant the boat had less chance of survival. This was especially true when one day, the workers noticed a crack running down the center of the boat's hull.[3] The parched wood was beginning to warp—the dryness everyone could readily see on the surface was penetrating the wood all the way through. It seemed that even if the boat appeared to hold together until the pool could be flooded, it might still be too late to save it.

Incredibly, it took the same amount of time to excavate the boat from the polyurethane as it took to rescue it from the mud. Eleven days after the craft had successfully been lowered by crane into the preservation tank, the final remnants of the polyurethane foam had been stripped from the wood. It was a time to celebrate when pumps were turned on and steadily poured water into the pool, but it was also an anxious time. There was a good chance the boat had been almost totally dried out by the sun. It was certainly showing plenty of signs of dehydration.

If the vessel rose with the water level in the pool, then a new plan would have to be formed. There was a small chance that the boat could be weighed down, but if the wood was totally dry, then the crew would run into the same issue with buoyancy as had faced them with the polyurethane. As the water reached the bottommost part of the keel, everyone was as nervous as a college freshman on finals day. By the time the water rose above the top of the planking, there was no one present without a huge smile across his face. The ancient boat hadn't budged from the bottom of the pool.

Once the boat had been submerged in water, it didn't stay that way every day. It certainly sat in the pool soaking up as much moisture as it could each night, but during the day the excavators, now conservators, had to prepare the boat for the preservation phase. In one of the presentations given at the United States Embassy in Herzliya, a plea had been made on behalf of the boat because funding could not be procured through the Department of Antiquities for the PEG that the project so desperately needed. After discussing the problem with Bud Rock, the Science Attaché, he told them he would make some calls to various chemical companies. After a few days' time, Shelley received a call from Bud saying that an Israeli Dow Chemicals distributor had agreed to donate the PEG for the boat's preservation.[4]

Having the synthetic wax donated for the conservation process was a substantial help for the team. Using PEG was the safest bet to preserve the boat. If they hadn't been able to get it for free, the conservators would possibly have had to go with another, less sure option. At the very least, they would have waited many years until the Department of Antiquities had room in its budget to purchase the PEG.

Thankfully, they didn't have to resort to either of those alternatives. With the PEG as good as in hand, they could start on the plan for preservation.

Because the cactus needles had gotten too soggy to hold the identification tags to the wood, metal straight pins had been used back at the initial excavation site. Over the short amount of time they had been in the wood, they had already begun to rust. They weren't suitable for long-term usage, especially since the PEG would react strongly with them and would probably dissolve them all. Identification tags needed to be kept on the boat, so more durable pins had to be located.

Nitza got in touch with a friend who ran a factory at another kibbutz by the Sea of Galilee. She explained the situation to him, and asked if he could help out the conservation with materials. The timing of the request could not have been better.

The factory in which the man worked created giant coiled spools of stainless steel wire. Somehow, one of these industrial coils had become tangled up in itself, spoiling the wire and making it useless for the purpose for which it had been intended. Since they could no longer use the wire, he immediately offered to give the entire spool to the conservation of the boat. The conservators could not have asked for a better material.

Where the normal steel pins would have rusted and dissolved, the stainless steel wire would hold up against the potentially corrosive properties of the PEG. Using a simple pair of wire cutters, the wire could be clipped to the length needed for the task at hand. As the boat was being prepared for preservation, this turned out to be an extremely useful resource.

Over the course of both excavations, the already fragile timbers were put under a lot of stress that they had not had to face while buried in the mud. Between dehydration in the sun, transportation, and any accidental damage caused by the digging, some of the original joints had weakened and some timbers had begun to loosen.

Worried that these loose fragments of wood might fall off the boat while it sat in the wax bath, the conservators decided to fasten them in place. Putting the stainless steel wire to use once more, they clipped lengths off the spool in long enough segments to be bent like staples. They used these ad hoc staples to pin the loose pieces of wood in place, securing them against whatever the next few years would bring.[5]

While the team was working on the boat in the pool one day, they noticed something that struck them with horror. What they saw was actually a fascinating natural miracle, but it was hard to take it that way under such tense conditions. Sometimes, eggs and seeds can lie dormant for extremely long periods of time and will only begin to grow or hatch when the proper conditions finally present themselves. When the conservators submerged the boat in freshwater, they had unwittingly created the right growth conditions for a host of eggs.

When these eggs hatched, the pool was suddenly swarming with tiny, red mosquito larvae. The eggs likely had been in the wood since the boat was initially buried, so the mosquitoes that hatched were almost 2,000 years old. The people working in the water didn't care how old the larvae were. I don't know anybody who likes mosquitoes, and even if they weren't grown yet, the conservators still thought them a nuisance.

Besides the fact that the little red worms were pests, there was a chance that if these insects had survived, there could be other things waiting to come back to life inside the wood. Even though the mosquitoes would not damage the boat, it wouldn't be good to give anything that might eat the ancient wood a chance at life. Orna began looking into chemicals they could put in the water to kill any freeloaders.

The problems with that plan were twofold: On the one hand, the chemical had to be picked carefully so that it wouldn't damage the wood itself; on the other hand, there were still people working on the boat, and mixing chemicals into the water could be harmful to their health. While most of the crew was deliberating how to handle the situation, Moishele was one step ahead of them all. As I have said, he had been raised to be a fisherman, and he had spent his life on the shores of the Sea of Galilee. Growing up, he took time to watch the fish along the shoreline, and he had learned what each different kind of fish liked to eat. He had seen these kinds of larvae before, and he knew precisely what to do about the problem in the tank.

Moshele went to Orna to convince her that they should try using fish to eat the mosquito larvae. After all, if there were any problems it would be much easier to remove fish from the water than diluted chemicals! After hearing his idea, she thought it was worth a try. Once he got the go-ahead, Moishele went out with his father, Yant-she, to catch some fish for the tank.

On the following day, Moishele showed up with a few different kinds of fish. He brought a certain type of St. Peter's Fish (Amnun in Hebrew, Musht in Arabic) that he knew would happily eat the larvae. In addition to the St. Peter's Fish, he brought some goldfish and carp, bottom feeders. These fish actually kept the tank clean, in case anything started to grow in the water. The second two kinds of fish that he brought provided an added benefit that not even he had anticipated. The goldfish and carp actually swam over the surface of the boat, eating residue that had formed on the wood. Without even planning it, the fish spotlessly cleaned the boat for the conservators before the PEG was introduced into the tank. It turned out to be a huge blessing that Moishele had brought the fish to the pool.

As the boat was being prepared for its preservation, the right equipment had to be set up as well. Orna already knew that the wax would have to be kept hot, and the pool had been designed with that in mind. However, insulation alone wouldn't keep the PEG at a toasty 140 degrees. A system of wires, pumps, and pipes was devised to heat and clean the wax in the tank. To keep vibration from moving through the tank, a motor was set up at a short distance. This motor would drive two separate pumps to keep the wax moving in the pool and running it through filters to keep it clean. There were also 50 heating units lowered down the sides of the pool that would keep the wax at the proper temperature.[6]

The boat sat in its freshwater pool for two years while each system was designed and every piece of equipment was built. Since the boat was safely submerged in water there was no longer any fear of dehydration. The team of conservators had been able to take their time making sure everything was totally ready before the final stage was begun. The boat had been fully re-tagged and stabilized, and the elaborate system Orna designed for the PEG had finally been completed to her specifications.

At long last, the PEG started to arrive. Two different densities of the chemical were to be used during the course of the conservation: one with a high density and one with a low density. The low-density PEG would be used in the initial phase of preservation. Because of the different woods used in the construction of the boat, these different densities were necessary. The lower-density wax would interact well with some of the types of wood, whereas the higher density would be best for the other woods in the boat.

PEG wax begins to arrive at the museum

It was with the low-density PEG 600 that the preservation started. It was introduced into the tank in small increments daily, letting the synthetic wax replace the water as it evaporated in the tank's high temperature. Each day, as the ratio of PEG to freshwater grew, the liquid in the tank gradually went from being clear to looking rather dark, dirty, and opaque.

It smelled terrible. As the PEG mixed with the water, an overwhelming chemical stench started to rise from the pool. It wasn't poisonous, but it certainly wasn't going to make anyone happy, either. Because it was right beside the Sea of Galilee, there were frequent winds that would blow the smell from the tank over the kibbutz. There was no escape from the pungent odor when the winds were just right (or wrong). However, it was also the smell of the boat's salvation. If these chemicals hadn't been available, the boat would probably not survive.

Yuvi, for one, ran with that idea. He fell in love with the smell of the wax, which he speaks of today as a perfume. Everyone else hated it.

All aromas aside, this was the day that everyone had been waiting for. Now, for the most part, there was nothing more to do with the boat. The PEG would treat its timbers and, aside from someone checking on it every day and adding supplemental amounts of the wax into the pool, the process would run on its own. Everyone could finally take a breather.

Fail-safes had been set in place to protect the boat. In case of a power failure, a generator was hooked up, ready and waiting to provide power for the heating and the pumps if need be. Orna, who lives and usually works in Jerusalem, would come out to Ginosar a few times every week to check on the status of the boat. In her absence, one of the employees of the Yigal Allon Museum would be assigned to check on the pool every day. If anything went wrong, Orna would be notified immediately, and she would drop every-thing and come to the site.

In the meantime, however, it was only right that Orna, at long last out from under the immediate stress of her task, took a holiday.

Seemingly waiting just for the moment when she left, something went terribly wrong with the PEG. The water and wax solution began to ferment in the pool, filling with bacteria and putting the boat in immediate danger. True to form, as soon as she heard about the crisis Orna abandoned her vacation and rushed back to Ginosar. Once back, she contacted an expert on bacteria, and the two con-ferred as to how best solve the problem.

Although it was serious, it was fairly easy to take care of the situa-tion. The wax that had been introduced to the pool, along with all of the water, was pumped out. The whole pool was rinsed thoroughly, both the tank and the boat. Once all of the bacteria were hopefully flushed, the process was started again with a small concentration of PEG being added to the pool of water. The bacteria expert ran some tests on samples he had drawn from the contaminated water/wax mixture, and recommended a biocide for the pool so that a similar outbreak wouldn't occur again.[7]

After that, the low-density stage ran smoothly. For the following four years or so, the boat rested in water mixed with a progressively higher concentration of PEG. By the time the wax needed to be changed out with the higher-density PEG 4000, it was nearing the close of the year 1991. There was still a lot of time left in the project before the boat could be put on display, but it seemed everything was downhill from here.

To put the high-density PEG into the tank, the whole thing needed to be emptied and flushed. That took some time, but it allowed the workers to see the boat for the first time in years. No one had really been sure what the boat would look like—it had been totally submerged in dark, murky liquid that made it very difficult to see the boat. They had been trusting that the boat would survive the PEG treatment, and when it came time to swap the PEG, they saw their trust had been well placed. They also saw something fascinating in the wax they took out of the tank.

One of the fish that Moishele had brought to put in the tank with the boat had apparently not been fished out of the pool before the first batch of PEG was added. Completely unaware of what was going on, the little fish had continued to swim around in the pool as

The boat after one phase of PEG conservation

both the temperature rose dramatically and the water was replaced by wax. A few years later, it had been completely preserved by the PEG in the pool, as though it had been prepared by a taxidermist to be mounted as a trophy.

More importantly than the lone fish, though, the boat was revealed in the pool looking to be in better shape than when they had last seen it. Between the fish and the wax, the boat had been thoroughly cleaned, and any leftover mud had basically been stripped off by the years of chemical immersion. The wood looked so well preserved that it seemed almost fresh.

This was what the conservators had been waiting for—the chance to see the boat and make sure what they were doing was good for it. Clearly, it was. Such a sight was an immense relief for everyone. These were the same men and women who had toiled for eleven days to rescue the boat from the mud, and who had then had to re-excavate it from a cocoon of polyurethane. When they saw the boat after its first PEG treatment, every single person was sure that her exhausting labor in 1986 had been worth it. However, there wasn't a lot of time to stand around staring at the boat. It was photo-documented and its supports were reinforced to last through the coming, longer period of time in the higher density wax.

Having seen their beauty once again, it was time to start filling the pool with the PEG 4000. It had been delivered as a powdery solid, in 1,382 55-pound sacks. Since the pool had been flushed and emptied, it was necessary to melt down the PEG before it could be put into the pool. The problem was, in order to get the second phase of wax immersion underway, the conservators needed to put 10 tons, or 20,000 pounds, of PEG 4000 into the pool. That was a substantial amount, and would require a large tank in which to melt it down.

Once again, Moishele came to the rescue. At this point, he was working at Kibbutz Ginosar's ostrich farm, for which he used a large tank to provide the birds' water. Thinking on his feet, he got hold of the ostriches' tank and brought it to the site to melt the wax in. It was a rather lengthy process—they didn't have the means on site to melt the PEG down. What they wound up having to do was fill the water tank with as much powdered PEG as they could, nearly 1,700 pounds, and then use a tractor to drive it over to the kibbutz. Using the resources at the kibbutz's hotel, they added boiling water to the tank and mixed it until all the wax was melted. After that, it was back to the preservation pool, where the melted wax was pumped into the tank with the boat. After the initial trip, the whole thing had to be repeated a dozen times.[8]

They had to complete the task as soon as possible. The boat had to be immersed in liquid, so it was imperative that the PEG be melted down and put into the pool on the double. Moishele and Yuvi brought their family to help with the work, and with their help and the help of another kibbutznik, the job was finished by the end of the day.

From that point, the solid PEG could be added into the pool directly from the sacks to replace the water that evaporated. Since the pool was filled with hot PEG solution after that first day, the powdery wax added over time would melt once it mixed into the pool. Because the PEG used in the second phase was denser than the first batch had been, it was impossible to see anything in the swirling mixture. Visitors to the site had to be content with looking at a large pool full of dark liquid, but that seemed to be almost enough for them. There was a short video to watch explaining what happened during the excavation and I'm sure Yuvi and Moishele were more than happy to talk with tourists, but no one could see the boat itself.

At times it was difficult to believe the boat was still in the tank. Because it sat in hot chemicals for such a long time, it didn't take a vast leap of the imagination to picture broken chunks of wood, swirling around and slowly disintegrating. From time to time, even Orna had to satisfy her curiosity. To protect herself from the heat and the wax, she put on heavy-duty gloves and reached into the liquid to touch the boat. Every time she did that, though, its ancient timbers were just where she had left them.

The preservation process didn't go without any snags, of course. Problems weren't anywhere near as frequent as they had been during the excavation, but still things would happen that stopped everyone's hearts for a few moments.

The biggest one probably came one day when there was a short in the wiring that powered the heating units in the tank. Moishele had been visiting the boat, and felt his heart sink into his stomach when he noticed the wax was beginning to harden. At one in the morning, he went to Kurt and brought him to the boat.

They had to replace the faulty parts, but thankfully everything had been provided in case of an emergency. Before long the wax was heating up again, and it soon melted. The damage caused by that little short circuit was only measured in emotional and mental grief between the time Moishele first detected it and when he and Kurt got it fixed. The boat hadn't seemed to notice.

———

It took nearly an additional seven years to complete the preservation of the boat after the PEG 4000 had been added to the pool. It was 1998 by the time the team started to take the wax out of the tank for the final time. It had taken a few years longer than had initially been anticipated, but the wait had certainly paid off. The boat looked fantastic—the ancient timbers looked solid and in much better condition than they had been below the surface of the beach.

The two pumps now worked hard to extract as much wax from

the tank as they could. They pumped the hot liquid into separate containers that have been stored in the museum, in case any fragments of the boat had come off and been pumped out with the wax. The PEG was the color of burnt honey as it swirled around the deep brown of the boat's preserved timbers. Some of the wax that had been inside the boat wouldn't drain out, having gotten caught by the hull's interior. This excess wax had to be removed with any means at hand—mops and rags were used to absorb as much of the wax as was possible, and empty soda and juice bottles were filled with the liquid. The crew had to work fast, because once the wax cooled off and hardened, it would be much more difficult to remove the excess.

The boat was still as fragile as plate glass, despite however good it looked to the workers. Extreme care needed to be used even now when working on the boat, which would make removal of hardened excess wax difficult. In order to handle the situation delicately, a simple solution was the best solution, and so was put to use.

Hairdryers proved to be the most effective way to remove the wax from the boat. The hot air given off by these everyday appliances melted the excess wax. Once the wax had been melted, it was gently dabbed off the timbers with a rag. This process was labor intensive and required a lot of effort from volunteers and museum staff. It seems as though it wouldn't be terribly difficult to stand or even sit next to a boat, simply holding a hairdryer. It seems easy and straightforward, but it took hours a day to clear a patch of the wood. Imagine as well having to slide underneath the boat and melt the wax from the bottom of the hull—it dripped all over the workers, hardening in their hair and on their faces.

No one really seemed to mind, though. All the toil was freely undertaken as a labor of love—everyone involved with the boat's rescue, the whole process, considered it a joy to be able to work to save it. Even the newer members of the group who had joined in the work because of their employment at the museum were enthusiastic about the process, and there were no complaints from anyone.

Once the excess PEG had been satisfactorily removed from the boat's frame, it had to be left to dry. It took a day to make sure the boat had completely dried, but there were eyes on it the whole time. After so many years, seeing the boat sitting in the tank was like a dream come true. It looked as though it had only just been sunk that day.

All that remained for the boat now was to prepare it for display. It was in as good condition as it would ever be, and Orna only needed to make sure that the tank's climate was under control to keep it that way. The next task before the crew was to design a platform for the boat to rest on while it sat on display in the museum.

It was important that this platform be able to support the boat in such a way that the ancient craft's weight would be evenly distributed. By the time the design was decided, it was a contraption to behold. The whole thing was to be made of stainless steel. Two long pipes, like skis, would run down the middle of the boat, roughly imitating the curved line between the bow and stern and coming together at both ends. The pipes would stand on four legs, like a table. Attached to the top of the two central pipes would be fifteen support ribs, wider than the hull itself but basically conforming to the shape of the boat. The boat would not actually touch these ribs—there were 130 "fingers" reaching from the ribs to the wood, with small disks on their ends to present a greater surface for the ancient wood to rest on. Each one of the stainless steel "fingers" was designed for a specific place in the stand. They were constructed to particular lengths and the disks were affixed at exact angles so that they would properly support a precise part of the boat.

It was an elegant design, but it would take time to build and assemble. The measurements had to be exact—any variance, and the boat could shift and be impaled by the very stand designed to pro-

After years of sitting submerged in PEG, the boat is finally preserved

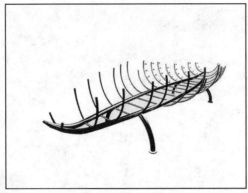

The final design of the boat's display stand

tect it. By the time it was ready, the new wing on the side of the Yigal Allon Museum would be ready as well, the new, permanent home of the miraculous boat.

Before the boat could begin its final journey, it had to be carefully packaged. This time, polyurethane was not an option—no one wanted to have to either cut it all off again or re-treat the boat. It was wrapped carefully in ordinary packaging material, and one last crane was hired to lift it into its new display room in the museum.

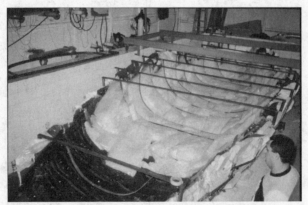

Workers package the boat for its final move

Left to Right: Chaim Herzog, former President of Israel; Jacques Mahfar;
Ruth Allon, Yigal's wife; Yitzhak Rabin, former Prime Minister of Israel;
Mula Cohen, former commander of a Palmach brigade

Yuvi stands on the beach over the boat

Kurt and Shelley have their first
look at the boat

A piece of the boat peeks out from the mud in front of a rainbow

Kurt and Yuvi look at the boat as the double rainbow arcs behind them

A clear view of the double rainbow

The excavation gets underway

Kurt surveys the clay cooking pot found by the boat

Groundwater fills the excavation site

Work halts on the boat as the dike is constructed

A truck sinks into the soft mud, momentarily slowing down progress

Kurt stands thinking in the Sea of Galilee

The dike completed, excavation continues on the boat

A backhoe is employed to enlarge the pit around the boat

Excavators stop to look at additional fragments of wood uncovered by the backhoe

The backhoe makes the process go faster

A camera crew tries to find the best angle to shoot from

Orna tries to stabilize the stern section with a polyurethane fill

A volunteer with a spray bottle tries to keep the wood from drying out

Moishele builds the hanging platform

Yuvi and another excavator work from the platform

*The first polyurethane is sprayed
into the boat at night*

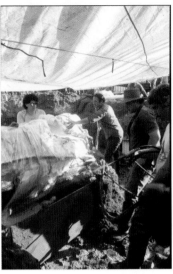

*A tunnel is filled with
polyurethane foam*

*Excavators lie on their stomachs in the mud to dig
tunnels under the boat*

Ready to fill the second half of the tunnels

Orna climbs on top of the boat as water fills the excavation pit

Sailing on the Sea of Galilee after 2,000 years in the mud

A motorboat is tied to the boat for the trip to the Yigal Allon Museum

Preparations are made to lift the boat back onto land

The boat is lowered into the conservation pool

Orna works to re-excavate the boat in the tank

Workers remove the polyurethane foam from the boat

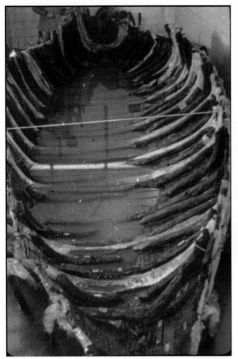

A view of the boat after its first PEG treatment

The boat's interior after the low density stage of PEG immersion

Draining the high density PEG from the pool after years of treatment

Packaging the boat for its final move

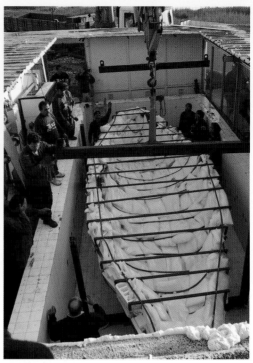

The frame is assembled to lift the carefully packaged boat

The crane eases the boat toward the opening in the wall

The boat finally enters the museum

A crew guides the boat to its final display location

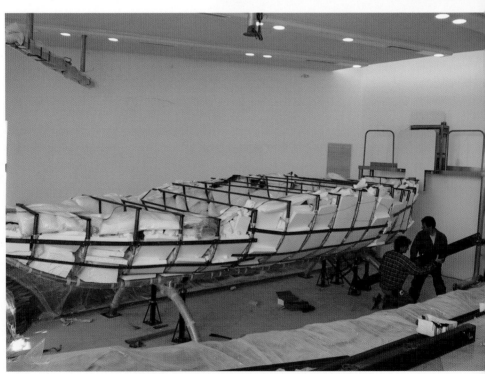

Workers finish putting the display stand together

TOP: *After exactly 14 years, the boat sits intact in a special wing of the Yigal Allon Museum*

MIDDLE: *A head-on view of the fully preserved fishing vessel*

BOTTOM: *A woman stands alone, looking at the boat from the time of Christ*

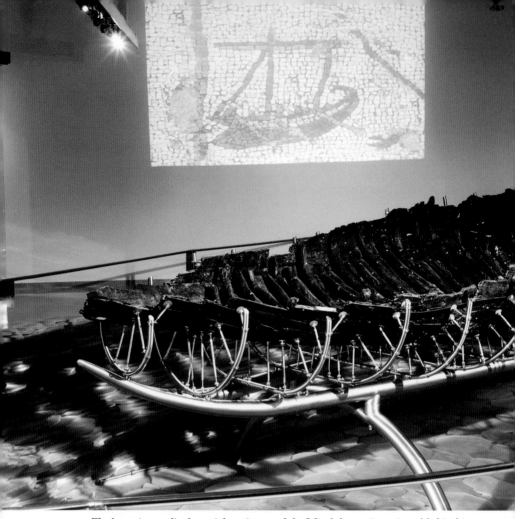

The boat sits on display with a picture of the Migdal mosaic projected behind it

The exhibit room

A narrative photo-display on the wall behind the boat

Close-up view of a mortise and tenon joint

A scale model of the Jesus Boat set against the Sea of Galilee

The Yigal Allon Museum

*A tour group on a full-size model
of the ancient boat*

*A diagram indicating the type
and location of the twelve woods
used in the boat's construction*

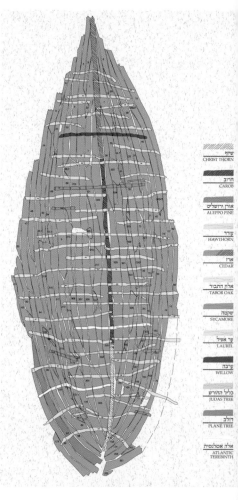

שיזף
CHRIST THORN

חרוב
CAROB

ארן ירושלים
ALEPPO PINE

עוזרר
HAWTHORN

ארז
CEDAR

אלון התבור
TABOR OAK

שקמה
SYCAMORE

עץ אצל
LAUREL

ערבה
WILLOW

כליל החורש
JUDAS TREE

דולב
PLANE TREE

אלה אטלנטית
ATLANTIC
TEREBINTH

The mouth of the Jordan River as it leaves the Sea of Galilee

After so much time and money had been spent on it, no risks were going to be taken. Needless to say, the crane operator who had initially tried to move the boat into the preservation tank was not offered the job.

On the day of the move, the boat was fully wrapped in white packaging, an attempt to keep it safe from any bumps or jostling it might encounter in its last voyage. The crane came to the site and, planting its legs securely in the ground, began to hoist the boat into the air. For the very last time, the boat rose and swiveled over all the workers' heads, and the crane operator positioned it in front of the museum. A large section of wall had been left open, and so the crane's arm extended into the building, the boat hovering over the floor of its new home. Once the boat floated over the display site, the crane stopped and workers rushed in to begin putting the elaborate stand together.

They all knew what they were doing, and before long the display stand was constructed. The crane's arm began to lower, and a hush ran through the room as the boat was slowly and carefully guided into place by some of the workers. All of a sudden, the boat was down. It had come to rest in its final home at last. The rush of

The boat is guided into place inside the museum

emotion, the euphoria at seeing the fruition of such a long endeavor come to pass, filled the museum.

Two men had brought bottles of champagne. Stacks of small paper cups were passed around the room, and the men with champagne shook their bottles and popped the corks. Everyone stood around, laughing and holding their cups up to catch the champagne as it sprayed from the bottles. Here, after so long, they had finished what they had set out to do. The packaging was removed with excitement from the boat, and as everyone had hoped nothing had damaged the ancient vessel in its final move. The boat had been saved!

The date was February 16th, 2000, exactly fourteen years to the day since the excavation had begun.

LUKE 5: 4–9

Trusting God In Every Situation

And when he had finished speaking, he said to Simon, "Put out into the deep and let down your nets for a catch." And Simon answered, "Master, we toiled all night and took nothing! But at your word I will let down the nets." And when they had done this, they enclosed a large number of fish, and their nets were breaking. They signaled to their partners in the other boat to come and help them. And they came and filled both the boats, so that they began to sink. But when Simon Peter saw it, he fell down at Jesus' knees, saying, "Depart from me, for I am a sinful man, O Lord." For he and all who were with him were astonished at the catch of fish that they had taken.[1]

It isn't always easy to follow God's commands, especially when a lot of people are watching. Often people will feel they know exactly what they ought to be doing, only to hear God's voice telling them to do exactly the opposite. When that happens, not only is it confusing but it can also be embarrassing.

When Peter hesitated to let down the nets for one last attempt, he had good reason. He had been working presumably for hours, and to come back with nothing to show for your effort after so long can be extremely frustrating. He and his partners were exhausted from a long night of hauling in empty, weighted nets.

Sick of failing, he had returned to shore only to find a man preaching by the water. He kindly agreed to let the man enter the boat so

149

that he could more comfortably speak to the large crowd pressing around him.

While Jesus preached to his audience, his words clearly made an impression on Peter as well. By the time the sermon was finished and Jesus asked his host to sail back out and try for one last cast of the nets, Peter was calling him "master" and agreed to do as was suggested. Perhaps the tired fisherman simply wanted to humor this captivating speaker so that he could get rid of him, or possibly somewhere deep in his heart he wanted to trust that maybe, just maybe this last attempt would work.

Regardless of the motive, he took his boat back out toward the deeper parts of the lake to lower the nets just once more. He probably had to swallow quite a bit of pride to turn the boat around. As a hard-bitten fisherman, he knew that a long night's worth of fishing isn't going to suddenly improve without reason. This man in his boat, while eloquent, clearly wasn't a fisherman. Surely Peter knew more about fishing than this Jesus did.

Besides that, he had come in to shore with an empty boat, only to land near a large crowd of people. In a fishing community, people would have known the look of a crew that has been unsuccessful all night long, and Peter surely had that wearied look etched all across his face. If, after following Jesus' suggestion he returned to the harbor once again with an empty boat, how foolish would he look to everyone on shore? How much more foolish would he feel?

Imagine his surprise when he felt an incredibly strong resistance against the net when he tried to pull it up! Not only had this man Jesus just accurately predicted a catch of fish, it was the largest catch Peter had ever seen! It was so big that he had to call the other boat (probably the boat pulling the other side of the seine net) closer so that they could load up all the fish into the two vessels.

One thing is for sure: Peter had to have been extremely glad that he decided to listen to Jesus' suggestion. Against the odds and despite how dumb he could have looked if Jesus had been wrong, he decided to trust the strange preacher. His trust paid off with incomparable returns.

8

꙰

By The Shores
Of Galilee

The entire excavation process was an amazing time in which
everyone involved sacrificed his time and efforts to rescue the
boat. Everything came together as it was needed; it truly seemed to
be the hand of God working with the excavators to ensure that the
boat made it through the various stages of excavation and conservation. One of the greatest parts of the story of the boat's rescue, however, is one that nobody seems to pay much attention to. Needless
to say, without the people who spent their time working at the site,
the boat would not have made it.

However, the specific individuals who were part of this extraordinary discovery were invaluable and irreplaceable. The whole sequence
of events hinged on the people who made it run, and it was only the
particular combination of men and women who were there through

the excavation and remained for the conservation process that, with God's help, allowed the boat to survive and be put on display.

It cannot be stressed enough that the timing of every single event surrounding the boat's rescue from the Sea of Galilee was perfectly orchestrated by God to let the ancient fishing vessel survive. This includes the people involved in the process. Without Orna and Shelley, Kurt, Moishele, and Yuvi, the boat would not have made it to the Yigal Allon Museum. Without the additional help of the Kinneret Authority and Ambassador Pickering, the materials and funding necessary to complete the project would not have been available.

Without the untiring support of Kibbutz Ginosar, the frenzied pace the excavation was required to follow would have been impossible. From the time Yuvi and Moishele, sons of the kibbutz, found the boat, the kibbutzniks "adopted" it and decided to do whatever they could to aid the dig.

Every night, after a full day's work, the kibbutz held a meeting to determine whether to continue to support the excavation. Because of the long days spent at the beach digging out the boat, these kibbutz meetings could not meet before midnight or 1 a.m. The result of these late-night conferences was always the same—the kibbutz decided, without hesitation, to support the dig.

Their support came in incredible ways. Everyone who was able to work at the actual excavation site put in two shifts of work each day, to make sure the work got done. Not everybody was able to work at the site, though. Some people were too old, some too young, and others simply had too many responsibilities at the kibbutz to spend almost two weeks away from their duties. These people, while they couldn't be present at the excavation, physically digging in the mud, provided help in any way possible.

Having an excavation that goes all day leaves little time for the workers to prepare meals. During all the hours of sunlight and even into the night, the excavators were hard at work on the boat. They couldn't spend time preparing meals or occasional snacks along the way in case anyone got hungry. With the high level of energy they were using in the hot sun, tiring out their muscles digging countless pounds of mud and clay every day, the crew at work on the boat required nourishment to replenish the energy they spent at the site.

That's where the other kibbutzniks came in. Keep in mind that Nahsholim, Kurt's kibbutz on the Mediterranean coast, required him to come back every day to perform his chores. That isn't a bad thing—kibbutzim are founded on communal principles, and Nahsholim was simply maintaining its policy that all active members are required to pull their own weight. Ginosar, however, wanted to do everything in its power to aid the boat's rescue. That meant that the people who were at work on the boat might not be able to do their daily chores at the kibbutz. The people who remained at the kibbutz each day took care of those duties so that the kibbutz could still function properly. In addition to that aid, many of the members of Ginosar prepared cakes and sandwiches so that those working on the boat didn't go hungry.

Everyone from Ginosar pitched in and did what she could to keep the excavation afloat. Men, women, and children volunteered their time and effort in whatever way they could and made sure that the job got done. The kibbutz couldn't provide everything, though. There were certain resources for which the excavation team had to look elsewhere for, and one of those places was the American Embassy.

Thomas Pickering, American Ambassador at the time of the excavation, proved to be the right diplomat at the right time. His personal enthusiasm for archaeology attached him deeply to the project, and he did everything in his power, including pulling some very important strings, to help the excavators save the boat.

During the course of the excavation, Pickering created opportunities for the work on the boat to continue at full speed. He was the one who gave approval for the funding for Steffy's last-minute transatlantic flight. He was responsible for setting up the presentations that Shelley and Kurt gave at the embassy. Every day, Ambassador Pickering would ask the two archaeologists what they needed for the project. Whatever they told him, he did his best to get them in front of the people who could supply the necessary tools and funding.

Pickering hosted pool parties for corporate bigwigs and executives in the industries that could be beneficial for the excavation. Dow Chemicals, for example, was made aware of the boat by Pickering's hard work, and as a result of that the company supplied the crew with a synthetic wax necessary for the boat's conservation. Pickering understood the significance of the boat, both for the worlds of archaeology and of faith. Consequently, he went out of his way to find out what the excavation needed and provided as much as possible.

It seems that all of the major participants in the excavation were handpicked by God to play their particular roles in this incredible story. Many of the crew were born and raised in the area; like the Lufan brothers, they were deeply rooted in the Sea of Galilee and the lands surrounding it. Others like Richard Steffy were only part of the community for a short while. Others still had uprooted from their former lives and transplanted themselves in Israel, drawn by the beauty and the history.

Kurt Raveh was one of the latter. He is Dutch by birth, and grew up in the Netherlands. Spending his early years in the Netherlands, Kurt was constantly around water. He lived in a coastal town whose motto was "live by the sea, die in the sea." Fishing and maritime travel was an important part of the lifestyle in Kurt's hometown, and so it was a natural choice for him to become a nautical archaeologist.

There were a few bumps in the road along the way to becoming an archaeologist, however. When he was sixteen, Kurt went to the Dutch naval academy and was sent to South America upon graduating. Following his military service, Kurt stayed near the region with KLM and was based mostly in the Caribbean. During this time, he was in a helicopter crash in a jungle, and he and his fellow survivor began talking about Israel (Kurt had the Star of David on his equipment). Following their rescue, the two men made a vow that one day they would go to Israel.

By the time Kurt and his friend made it to Israel, it was just prior to Yom Kippur, 1973. The war that broke out between Egypt, Syria, and Israel on Yom Kippur saw everyone pressed into service to defend the Jewish State, and in order to get into the country the two men had to work in a kibbutz. The war went on for about three weeks, but Kurt had fallen in love with the country. He ended up staying much longer.

Coming from the Caribbean, Kurt felt that the Israeli Mediterranean coastline was the most beautiful land he had seen, and decided to buy a house and live there. He joined Kibbutz Nahsholim, and married one of the kibbutz's daughters. Living by the Mediterranean Sea, Kurt was finally able to fulfill his life's dream—excavating shipwrecks. "Every [nautical] archaeologist hopes to find, once in his lifetime, a shipwreck," Kurt said. "We found everything! I don't even have a wish list anymore." So far, he and his colleagues have found over 100 shipwrecks—there are 28 in the bay by his house alone.

Even with all of these discoveries, there are still a few things that Kurt is missing—a fedora, a leather jacket, and a whip. His friends call him Indiana Jones, an appropriate nickname. Kurt told me some of the adventures he has had while looking for antiquities underwater. While he hasn't had to stop any evil men with aspirations to take over the world, there have been occasions in which he has almost died. It may sound cliché, but he has stories of dives in which his life has literally flashed before his eyes, like a movie.

I asked Kurt what his favorite discovery was. He said that the greatest project he had ever worked on was the ancient boat from the Sea of Galilee. Despite the dozens and dozens of shipwrecks he has found, more than any warship or chest full of gold, this small, inconspicuous hull of a fishing boat has the most significance for him. This boat was the one boat he hoped to find, just once in his lifetime.

He wasn't alone in that. Yuvi and Moishele, the ones who got the whole project going, were the two men who had actually spent their lives dreaming of finding this boat.

These two brothers are truly the salt of the earth from Jesus' ministerial base. While the world has gone on and changed dramatically from the time Christ preached the Good News to the Jews, fishermen have stayed fairly consistent with their New Testament counterparts. Yuvi no longer works as a fisherman, but Moishele still carries on the family tradition.

Fishing in the Sea of Galilee has started to change, and some of the old methods, such as the seine net, are no longer used as they once were. Motorized boats now ply the waters of the Sea of Galilee, disturbing the tranquility of the lake. Moishele, as a fisherman, dislikes the way the current fishing industry is run. After the ancient boat was pulled out of the mud and studied, tour boats on the lake now look like the boats of the first century A.D., but Moishele wants more.

A true fisherman, Moishele wants a return to the way fishing used to be done—a boatful of men hauling in nets, without the clatter of loud motors and stench of diesel fuel filling the air. The care Moishele has for the boat is an outworking of the admiration he has for the Sea of Galilee. He wants to see the lake restored to its ancient beauty, without all of the trappings of modern life spoiling it. To him, the boat is a gift that allows everyone today to see how fishing and watercraft used to be on the Sea of Galilee. Moishele's dream today is to bring back the honor of fishing to the Sea of Galilee.

His older brother Yuvi is not quite the same as Moishele. Yuvi used to be a fisherman—for a time, he moved down to Eilat, the southernmost point of Israel jutting into the Sinai Peninsula. He moved back to Ginosar because he couldn't live without the smell of fish and the smells of the lake flooding his nostrils every day when he went to the Sea of Galilee's shores. Ever since the boat was discovered, though, Yuvi has become someone totally new.

Yuvi followed a childhood love of art to become a resident artist at Ginosar. He still loves the Sea of Galilee and spends as much of his time by its shores as he can, but much of his time is now occupied with his sculptures that can be seen all around the kibbutz. His stonework exhibits his love of wordplay, and thus it comes as no surprise that the discovery of the boat has had another profound impact upon his life.

"I used to be a fisherman, but now I am a fisher of men." Raised in a kibbutz—a secular settlement, remember—it is a bit shocking that he has an affinity for this saying, and even more so that he sees it directly applying to his own life. Yuvi does, however, believe that the boat was given to him and his brother for a reason, and that God was orchestrating the entire excavation. That makes sense, seeing as how it was so frantic and disorganized; yet it all came together perfectly to accomplish what no one thought possible.

These are just some of the people who were involved in the boat's rescue, and they were all responsible for its continued survival. It has already been said that Kurt and Shelley gave up their free time, even to the detriment of health and personal safety, in order to make the dream a reality. Everyone, however, who was part of the excavation and recovery process, threw himself wholeheartedly into the endeavor.

Kurt has lived in an Israeli kibbutz for 35 years and he said that he has never seen a kibbutz come together like Ginosar did to save the boat. Most kibbutzim are concerned with their own management, and don't care about what goes on outside the community. If it doesn't concern the kibbutz, then the kibbutz isn't concerned about it.

The way that Ginosar rallied around the boat was unlike anything Kurt or any of the other excavators had seen before. This boat really had nothing to do with the kibbutz at all; nonetheless, any sacrifice that could be made to help out the excavation was made without the slightest hesitation.

Because of their unflagging zeal for the boat's good, even at their own expense, Kurt, Shelley, and the other excavators fought for the boat to be put on display at the Yigal Allon Museum (Nitsa had by this point agreed that the boat ought to be displayed there). Some of the officials in the Department of Antiquities wanted to have the boat put on display in larger museums, such as the National Museum in Haifa or the Israel Museum in Jerusalem, but Kurt was adamant.

The people of Ginosar had done so much to care for the boat during the excavation that Kurt was convinced that once it was in a museum, no one would care for it as well as they would. After all, when even the Department of Antiquities couldn't support the excavation because it didn't have the budget, the kibbutz made every necessary sacrifice to bring it out of the mud.

Kurt's argument was convincing, and it was agreed that the boat would be displayed at Ginosar. It turned out that had the decision gone another way and the boat was sent somewhere other than the Yigal Allon Museum, it probably would not have survived. Even today, after the conservation process has been completed, the boat is extremely fragile and could break as easily as if it had been made out of glass. If an attempt at long-distance transportation had been undertaken, even just to Jerusalem, it was as likely as not that when it came time to unwrap and display the boat, only broken fragments of hull would have remained in the transport container.

The boat still has a strong following at the kibbutz. Many of the community members go in to look at it occasionally, but it has some more regular visitors as well. Orna, who now lives in Jerusalem, drives north to the Sea of Galilee to check on the boat a few times a month. She is still in charge of maintaining its condition, and at the slightest indication that there is a problem she flies to Ginosar to check on it.

Moishele, who for some years lived near Haifa rather than Ginosar, made the long drive out to see his brother and the boat two or three times a week. His heart had developed a special place for the ancient boat, even though there wasn't much work at all for him to do on it anymore.

Yuvi, perhaps, is the most attached to the boat. He did, after all, dream all his life of finding it. Even when the chances of the boat being destroyed were greater than it surviving, Yuvi always trusted that no harm would befall it.

I had the privilege to be at the museum with Yuvi one day as a large group of tourists from around the world watched a short video presentation on the excavation. After it was done, the tour guide, who knew Yuvi, introduced him to her group. Yuvi told them the whole story, in a rather condensed form, of course. As he spoke, he welled up with emotion, and in his eyes you could see the entire excavation flooding back to his memory.

None of the people who worked on the excavation were left quite the same once it was over. The project left an indelible mark on their lives—for some it is that they are still involved in the ongoing work necessary to keep the boat in good condition; for others it's the relationships that were formed during the harrowing time spent saving the boat. For others still, it was the turning point that led many non-spiritual people to believe that there was some force at work that helped them protect the fragile boat.

Even though most of the people who worked at the excavation were atheists, there were too many miracles involved in the project from start to finish for them to simply explain away. From almost any perspective you can think of, this boat should not have survived. The rapidity and success with which the mounting obstacles were overcome is an unmistakable indication that something out of the ordinary was involved with this boat, and that is a fact that few if any of the excavators will deny today.

There is one additional mark that this ancient boat has left on the community in which it was found, and in which it still resides. The Yigal Allon Museum, as I have said before, was to be and predominantly is a museum dedicated to social history in Israel, and primarily in the Galilee region. The man after whom it is named, Yigal Allon, was a general in the Israeli War of Independence, but he dreamed of peace between Israelis and Arabs. He wanted the land to be shared between both peoples, so that everyone could celebrate their heritage and background.

In 1976, Allon established a peace conference called the Spring Gathering in Ginosar. It met every year until his death in 1980, at which point it stopped. Following the boat's conservation and its placement in the museum, the Spring Gathering was re-established. Every spring since 2002, Arab and Israeli high school and college students have met at the center, working together on creative projects and allowing for open discourse between the groups.

Truly, this boat has been a miracle for Ginosar, and those who have called it the "peace boat" or the "love boat" aren't far off the mark. Besides the peace conference, the animosity between Ginosar and Migdal evaporated just as easily as the water in the boat threatened to do. Astonishingly, coming together over this boat almost completely erased an ongoing rivalry the two settlements had had for years. The boat finally gave them all a common cause to rally around. And wouldn't you know it, by working together they were able to get the job done

9

☽

MIRACLES, MIRACLES, MIRACLES!

It is hard to pay close attention to the story of this boat and not have a sense of the miraculous that is associated with it. In other accounts of this story, some of these miracles have been acknowledged; others merely pass them off as coincidence, denying God's hand in what happened.

When talking about almost anything in Israel, it is hard to divorce the tangible from the supernatural. Israel is the cradle of two of the world's great monotheist religions (Judaism and Christianity), and has significance for Islam as well. The Bible is full of miracle accounts, and most places in that country are connected in some way or another with a piece of religious history.

Those who worked to save the boat in 1986 were not left untouched by the sense of the miraculous that surrounded this boat. Atheist archaeologist Shelley Wachsmann, who was part of the excavation and conservation crew from the very beginning, has written a book about the events concerning the boat in which he took part. His book is full of phrases in which he acknowledges that Providence had a hand in the rescue of this boat. He cites coincidences that are just too perfect to believe. There are even (possibly unintended) passing references made to God's watch over the crew and the excavation, the irony of which coming from an atheist is remarkable.

In one anecdote Wachsmann relates, the crew spends time occasionally checking the mud in and around the boat for artifacts with a metal detector. While few artifacts were ever recovered inside the boat, there was one coin that turned up, a 1986 U.S. penny, fallen by chance into the mud.

The significance of this anecdote comes in the final sentence, a remark made by Wachsmann in passing. "In God We Trust," the inscription on the penny's back, made enough of an impression on Shelley to merit its insertion into his book. I doubt that he, even in including that statement, understood the significance of those four words. For the entire process of uncovering and preserving this boat, the crew needed to trust in God. They were faced with the impossible, but God had given them this boat to protect, and God made sure that after surviving for 2,000 years, it would survive conservation.

The miracles surrounding, or maybe comprising, this story are overwhelming. In all accounts of the arduous task the crew faced in digging the boat out of the mud in which it had been entombed for 2,000 years, everything fell into place perfectly, and then some. From the very outset, it seems as though God brought everything together, allowing the impossible to come true as nobody could have expected, or even hoped.

The drought that Israel had been through in the year leading up to the discovery of the boat by the Lufan brothers was truly just the beginning of the miraculous events that followed. A drought is always a serious problem, especially in such a dry land as Israel. Having to drain the waters of the Sea of Galilee in order to provide water for agriculture could hardly have seemed like a good thing to anyone in Israel, especially as it has been noted that national morale ebbs and rises with the level of the Sea of Galilee. The fledgling state of Israel was only a few decades old, and it had been fighting for its survival all the while. Now, it faced an enemy about which it could do almost nothing—nature. A certain level of frustration, even despair, must have been entering the public consciousness. Against enemies with guns, at least a pitched battle could be fought. The outcome could, to some extent, be controlled. When faced with a drought, though, Israel was next to helpless as it relied on reserves and imported water.

Despite the fact that the drought brought no rain clouds, it definitely had a silver lining.

Without the drought, certainly the boat would not have been found. Without the drought, the double rainbow that Shelley Wachsmann, Kurt Raveh, and Yuval and Moshe Lufan saw when the two archaeologists confirmed the boat to be ancient would not have had as much poignancy as it did. Not only did the double rainbow—rare and amazing in itself—indicate God's blessing or approval for the boat's excavation, but the rain that accompanied it provided the first refreshment for the land in months.

It is interesting to note that, in finding an ancient boat with biblical connections, the sky should have opened up and a rainbow should have resulted. The rainbow, indicative of God's promise to never again flood the earth and destroy almost all life, was initially related to Noah's ark. Now, thousands of years later, an ancient wooden boat had been found on the shores of the Sea of Galilee, a lake with immense significance for the Christian faith. This vessel must be of some consequence for God to have preserved it for so long and presented it in such a manner.

The fact that the sky broke open and poured out a supply of much-needed water, immediately after the archaeologists discovered proof that the boat was ancient, is too striking to be mere coincidence. The entire event sounds very much like the fulfillment of an Old Testament blessing prophecy, and it is more than fair to interpret it as God's blessing.

Nor was that the only rainbow to grace the excavation. In his book, Wachsmann relates an incident in which he and conservationist Orna Cohen were talking while at work on the boat one day. Not surprisingly, some people were a bit skeptical of the impression of miracles that was spreading at the site. Orna took the opportunity to comment to Wachsmann that with the harsh sunlight and lack of clouds in the sky, there was no likelihood of seeing any rainbows that day.

A few minutes later, a hose, connected to one of the pumps used to keep the groundwater from inundating the site, sprung a leak. Almost immediately, men from the Kinneret Authority were taking care of the problem. I walked over and watched as it released a fine mist into the surrounding air.

And in the mist was a miniature rainbow.[1]

While a rainbow formed in the mist from a broken hose might not be terribly miraculous, its timing was. A constant theme around the recovery efforts was that when there was a need, often from out of nowhere it would be addressed. Even when the need was one of belief, when there was skepticism about what was happening, it was answered promptly and definitively.

There was one other rainbow that is associated with this story, and this last one is perhaps the most miraculous of all. A rare complete double rainbow, especially since this one signified the end of a drought, should indeed be taken as a heavenly sign that the excavation of this ancient boat was blessed. Even more of such a sign, however, is the "moonbow" that Orna, the same one who was skeptical about Wachsmann's rainbow, saw one night on her way to the work site.

It was dark out as Orna was driving along the road down to the lake to get to work. She had been up at Safed, where her parents lived at the time, and was returning to the site. There was rain falling as she drove, and she happened to take a look out over the Sea of Galilee. Over the lake, to her complete astonishment, was a rainbow, at night! In total shock, she stopped her car and got out to look at it. She didn't even care that the rain completely soaked her—this was something she had to see.

Night rainbows, or moonbows, are extremely rare and require specific circumstances in order to occur. In order to have a moonbow, the moon must be lower than 42° in the sky; the lower the angle of the moon, the better the chances are of having a moonbow. It, of course, goes without saying that it must be dark out. Moonbows are much harder to see than rainbows because the light from the moon is fainter than that of the sun, so the less ambient light around, the better.

Just as with rainbows, of course, there must be rain falling to catch and reflect the light of the moon. Also, if there are too many clouds blocking out the moon's light, there won't be a moonbow. Because of all of these criteria that must be fulfilled perfectly, moonbows are much rarer than rainbows. The fact that Orna, who had been skeptical of the significance of the double rainbow, saw one driving back to the work site has to be seen as more than mere coincidence.

Celestial signs weren't the only way in which God blessed the excavation, though. Understandably, when dealing with fragile ancient wood that disintegrates if it dries out too much, there are bound to be problems with uncovering and preserving it. The way that everything about this boat "just happened" to develop the way it did, having every problem solved when it was most needed, is more than mere coincidence.

Moishele and Yuvi told me something very interesting about the whole excavation, what Yuvi calls the greatest miracle involved in the dig. The first archaeologist on the site, the one who said the boat certainly wasn't ancient, was actually one of the main reasons for the frenzied pace that allowed the excavation to be a success.

Once the media got wind of the story, it exploded and everybody wanted to see the boat and know more about it. The Turkish boat filled with gold that the Midgalites were after piqued everyone's curiosity, and the dig site was flooded with hopeful treasure hunters. The antiquities department had expressed a lot of interest in the boat, but because of a lack of resources and funding, the excavation had to be postponed for a number of months.

The overwhelming public interest in the boat and the threat that that interest posed to the boat was enough to get the antiquities department rolling. They understood that they needed to act fast and excavate, or else greedy fortune seekers would destroy an irreplaceable artifact.

The brothers are extremely grateful that, although not necessarily for the right motives, Avner Raban jumpstarted the Department of Antiquities. Without his leak to the media, the excavation would have taken months more to get under way. The situation with him serves to illustrate once more how in this excavation, God used unlikely tools to let His will be done.

Possibly the most miraculous part of this whole adventure is the historical timing of the boat's discovery. The excavation and conservation crew hardly had the materials available to them to save the boat, without it facing even more damage than time had already brought upon it. It was difficult for the crew to counter the myriad problems that presented themselves, but solutions were available nonetheless. While some of the techniques they used were unorthodox, everything seemed to fit together as perfectly as puzzle pieces, and through their efforts the impossible was achieved.

The timing was so miraculous because it really was the first point at which this discovery could have been made. Had there been a similar drought 100 years prior to the 1985–1986 one that had allowed the boat to be found, it would have been a disaster. Yes, it is true that the archaeological significance of the boat's survival and discovery would have been much the same, but within days of its exposure to the air, it would have dried out (much like it started to do in 1986) and disintegrated. There would have been no backhoes to help dig trenches, no fiberglass to create support ribs for the hull. It would have been much harder to work by night—probably, gas lamps would have had to be used to light up a nighttime work site, but they would not have been as easy to use as electrical lamps.

Certainly, once any boat had been uncovered and cleared from the mud, there would have been no way of preserving its fragile timbers from further decomposition. The PEG wax solution that Orna Cohen used to replace the water in the timbers would not have been available, and there was no way that a tank could be kept heated effectively for 14 years to ensure that the wax wouldn't solidify.

The specialists who flew in to Israel to come to the excavation site would not have been able to travel there fast enough to identify the boat's features before it was completely ruined; the excavators would not have even had the time to get word to any specialists before it would have been too late. Anyone who was in the area who might have been able to do a preliminary study on the boat would have had very little time, and it would have been rushed, as every day the boat would have shown more deterioration.

The miracle of this boat is only available to us today because it was found when it was. Had it been discovered a hundred, fifty, even twenty years earlier, the resources that were necessary to preserve the boat would have been unavailable, and an amazing archaeological and historical find would have been lost.

The methods used may not always have been traditional, but the ideas were used because nothing else was available. There were aspects of the dig in which the conservation crew were pioneers. Techniques had to be developed on the fly, and because frequently they were untested they were risky and could possibly have jeopardized the boat, but there were no feasible alternatives. Everything happened perfectly to ensure the boat's survival. As if it were an answer to a prayer, whenever something was really needed to save the boat, it was provided.

When the water level of the Sea of Galilee began to rise after the rains began again, the excavators petitioned the Kinneret Authority to have the water pumped out of the lake and put in other reservoirs around Israel. An impossible request—nobody would, in her right mind, ever ask for such a thing. As it turned out, it was an impossible request, but for a different reason. The amount of water flowing back into the lake was greater in volume than the amount of water the pumps would have been able to get out of the lake. Normally, this would have been a wonderful blessing for Israel, but now the rising water level was threatening to ruin any hoped-for excavation.

Because of the significance of the boat, however, the Kinneret Authority agreed to build a dike around the dig site to hold back the rising waters of the Sea of Galilee. Crews and machinery were provided for this task, and earthworks were thrown up that ensured the work could go on unimpeded. It turns out that the wall built to protect the boat was, no surprise, more providential than first anticipated.

God provided help in the eleventh hour, as hopes were starting to fade. The crew from the Kinneret Authority arrived to build the dike just as a sharkia began to blow. Had the Authority team been delayed another day, perhaps even just a few hours, the boat might have been destroyed by the driving wind and waves.

Certain personnel were crucial for the successful recovery and study of the boat. The fact that the approval for Richard Steffy to be brought on board could have gone through so quickly meant that someone was pulling the strings from up above. To get the money needed to fly him to Israel, they had to work through a bureaucratic morass to get approval, and time was of the essence. Within a matter of hours after talking with a contact at the American embassy, the money for the plane ticket was approved in what Wachsmann calls "a bureaucratic miracle."[2]

Having secured their specialist in ancient shipbuilding, the crew was able to commence excavation, but more problems were to follow.

On the first scheduled day of excavation, the team was presented with a problem that could not have been foreseen, one that had nothing to do with archaeological technicalities or funding.

The situation that arose when the armed man from Moshav Migdal came to guard the boat put more than just the boat at risk. While that problem was ongoing, there was a serious chance that a crew member or even a tourist might be seriously injured.

Faced with the threat of violence both to people and the boat, the excavators needed to find a resolution fast. Motivated by greed, an armed man could become a serious crisis. Thankfully the situation was peacefully resolved, and there were no further threats of violence at the dig site.

Later, an amazing thing happened. Many Migdalites, who had been acting hostile before the excavation had begun, arrived as volunteers and offered their time and equipment to help the excavators. The animosity and tension that had been so thick at the beginning of the dig had vanished: Now, all that was in the air was a spirit of togetherness as everyone worked diligently to save the boat.

Some of the crew working on the boat, astonished at the way everyone came together and worked side by side, nicknamed the boat the "Love Boat." Truly, the way that people shed their differences and joined their efforts for a common purpose was miraculous. The change from anger and guns had been effected in a matter of days, and no resentment remained. God's hand was truly in the excavation.

Some of the ideas that developed among the crew, those ideas that qualify as the unorthodox methods mentioned above, certainly came as a stroke of genius. Where nothing of the kind had been done before, the crew came up with ways to meet challenges that were innovative and inspired.

Countless experts in their fields were stumped as to how the boat could be safely transported from the excavation site to the conservation site at the Yigal Allon Museum. The military's suggested techniques were too risky; others straightforwardly stated that such a feat was impossible. Nobody believed that the boat, as fragile as it was, could be harmlessly transported in one piece.

It is at points such as this, when human wisdom is defeated and no answers can be found, that God's wisdom comes through.

The idea that came to the team to support the boat with fiberglass ribs and encase it in a protective (and buoyant) cocoon of polyurethane foam was outlandish. Who could have thought that such an unusual solution would have been the perfect fit for the situation?

God knew what was needed, at that moment, to make sure the boat made it to the conservation tank. God knew that, of all the various options available to the team, the most unusual solution, encasing the boat in solidifying foam, would be the best choice. Two men from Kibbutz Ginosar provided the additional support that would be required to hold the boat together.

In addition to the local expertise, members of Ginosar had perfectly timed connections that kept the project moving, such as the connection with the construction firm for the polyurethane foam. That the company agreed and was available to help on such short notice is amazing—everything came together as it was needed. Perhaps it is a bit different in Israel, but in the United States, trying to hire someone on short notice doesn't always work out very well. The hint of some divine string-pulling is strongly evident in this episode of the boat's story, as it is throughout the rest.

At this point in the excavation, everything was going along at full steam. The workers must have been exhausted from such long days working in the mud, but they were sustained. God gave them the strength to complete the task they had begun, the task He had set them.

MARK 4: 37–41

Putting Aside All Fear

And a great windstorm arose, and the waves were breaking into the boat, so that the boat was already filling. But he was in the stern, asleep on the cushion. And they woke him and said to him, "Teacher, do you not care that we are perishing?" And he awoke and rebuked the wind and said to the sea, "Peace! Be still!" And the wind ceased, and there was a great calm. He said to them, "Why are you so afraid? Have you still no faith?" And they were filled with great fear and said to one another, "Who then is this, that even the wind and the sea obey him?"[1]

A common misconception about the storm in this passage is that it was a raging storm with 12-foot seas crashing over the boat. Many artists have painted pictures of the disciples frozen in fear as a huge wave is about to swamp their ship, while Jesus peacefully sleeps behind them. Thankfully, we can correct that image.

We must first remember the setting of the story: The Sea of Galilee. The phrase Mark uses to describe the scene is "a great windstorm," which in the context of the Sea of Galilee can with some assurance be taken to be the same storm as the modern sharkias. These storms are violent, it is true, but they are not as wild and turbulent as we might imagine.

Instead of 12-foot seas, waves in the Sea of Galilee get to be a bit higher than 3 feet during a sharkia, but not much more than that. Winds sweep across the lake at 30 mph or so—fast enough to waterski, but definitely not hurricane-force winds. Once you hear what the storms on the Sea of Galilee are actually like, they don't seem as though they would be too terrifying. They might make someone seasick, but they probably wouldn't sink a boat.

But that's in a modern boat. The boats in the first century A.D. were fairly small due to limited resources, and thanks to this discovery we know exactly how small they were. If we imagine, as the account in Mark tends to make people think, that the boat contained all twelve apostles in addition to Jesus, that means the boat was just about at its maximum capacity. Such a full boat would have been riding low in the water, and if it sank, the swim to shore could have been over a mile, in a raging storm no less.

The Gospel narrative says that the waves were already crashing over the sides of the boat, and that the craft was taking on water. In a boat completely full of men, the growing water weight was a bad thing. If this had continued, it was only a matter of time before the boat would be swamped and it would be every man for himself.

The disciples' fear seemingly was rather well earned. In addition to their terror at their situation, they had a man sleeping through the whole ordeal. In their minds, it was more than fair that they wake Jesus up so he could help, seeing as panicked as they were.

When he was woken, they did not get the response they were expecting. Jesus showed no fear, only anger that the disciples had lacked the faith in him to put aside their fear and trust in God.

Mark writes that after Jesus calmed the seas, his disciples "were filled with great fear." He makes no explicit mention of their fear before this point—it only needs to be assumed in such a situation. Now, however, they were greatly afraid.

One of the most frequent commands spoken by Jesus was not to be afraid or anxious. In the course of the Gospel narratives, this instruction is reiterated, driving the point home: We are not to fear. As it is written in 1 John 4:18, "perfect love casts out fear." If we truly love and trust in the Lord, we will not fear when circumstances seem to be going against us.

Mark 4: 37–41 is a wonderful lesson for Christians at any time. When faced with a threat, even the threat of death, we are not to worry. Just as Jesus was present in the boat with the disciples then, so he is present with us today.

God has more than enough power to rescue us from any terrifying situation. The question is: Do we have enough faith to believe that?

10

MAKING WAVES

The discovery of this boat has been called one of the greatest archaeological discoveries of the twentieth century. This is not an overstatement. This boat, the only one of its kind to have survived in the Sea of Galilee, provides us with a connection to Jesus' ministry around that lake that we previously did not have.

During the time of the boat's life on the lake, the period of Jesus' ministry, the surrounding region was not terribly wealthy. The Sea of Galilee was plied mainly for fishing. Merchants' vessels may have crossed it as well, but the boats in use would have been built for an entirely practical purpose, not for pleasure cruising. There simply was not an abundance of wealth either in that place or at that time. The boat's construction, certainly, points to this fact.

It was repaired countless times, an obvious attempt to get it to last as long as possible before a replacement boat had to be built.

This alone is definitely indicative of its owner not being wealthy. Had the boat's owner or owners had plenty of money at their disposal, the boat would have been built with good materials, both for the initial construction as well as later repairs.

Studying the boat's construction, it isn't difficult to see that the boat was made with low-quality supplies. On top of that, the dozen different kinds of wood used in the hull's structure show that the builder was forced to use whatever he could find at hand, not typical kinds of lumber.

All this serves to indicate that whoever used this boat didn't have a lot of money. It's won't hurt to summarize what is known about the boat before drawing any conclusions. We also know almost certainly that this was a fishing boat and that it was in use around the first century A.D. With that in mind, it's a good idea to review an account of this time and place—the Gospels of the New Testament.

Remember that the Gospel writers were not novelists or historians. They didn't try to grasp people's imaginations with flashy physical descriptions or paint mental images of the cities about which they wrote. They were concerned with Jesus' life and ministry, not their surroundings.

None of the Gospel writers gives a detailed description of a boat. During the course of his ministry in the Galilee, Jesus is often depicted in and around boats, but we don't know what kind of boat or how large it was.

Traditionally it is assumed that all twelve of the apostles would have sailed in a boat together with Jesus, but that is never actually written explicitly. True, there are times that it seems to be the case, such as in Mark 4:36: "And leaving the crowd, they took him with them in the boat, just as he was." In the first half of this verse, it seems clear by virtue of the language that Jesus and the Twelve were together in a boat. However, the second half of the verse makes the idea a bit more ambiguous: "And there were other boats with him."

Were the other boats filled with the crowds that wanted to follow Jesus, or were they holding the spillover because the apostles couldn't all fit in the same boat as Jesus? In his book, Shelley Wachsmann made some quick calculations with the aid of some contemporary accounts of the Sea of Galilee courtesy of Josephus, a first-century Jewish historian. Based on the source he used, Shelley came to the conclusion that this boat, when in good shape, could have held at least fifteen men.[1]

There is a chance that the boats in Josephus' narrative are of a different construction than the boats that Jesus and his apostles would have used, but that chance is slim. Remember, in first-century ship construction on the Sea of Galilee the name of the game was practicality, not creativity. The best design, utilized for carrying passengers, freight, or fish, was one that would carry the most weight without sacrificing mobility.

It's almost certain that there would have been other kinds of boats, but not of this size. Smaller craft would have been used for various purposes—short trips, solo fishing—but the long hull found by Ginosar was probably typical of the larger boats on the Galilee at the time. There is no reason to believe that the ship with the high curving bow and two oars to a side depicted in the Migdal mosaic looked any different from the boat discovered by Moishele and Yuvi.

Each boat of this style, the large size, needed a crew of five to properly operate. It probably could have been manned with one sailor, but only if there was a constant wind. Otherwise, that one person could be left stranded in the middle of the lake in the event that the wind died down.

When Jesus called his first disciples, they left their fishing to come to him. Peter and Andrew were casting a net, probably standing in the shallows. When they heard Jesus, "immediately they left their nets and followed him."[2] James and John, however, were not fishing at the time Jesus appeared. They sat fixing nets in their boat. When they left to follow Christ, they "left their father Zebedee in the boat with the hired servants."[3] Because Mark indicated multiple servants with his plural usage, his readers can piece together the fact that there were at least five men in the boat when Jesus called James and John. Five people in a boat—perhaps one to an oar and one man to steer?

This means the boat discovered at Ginosar is the same kind of boat as that portrayed in the Gospels.

So what?

Of course, if there was only one style of boat in use on the Sea of Galilee during the first century A.D., it makes sense that this boat should be the same kind of boat as the disciples had. It's helpful to have some confirmation from the Gospels themselves.

So is it possible to determine whether or not Jesus was in any way connected to this boat? Strictly speaking, no, it isn't. However, this boat can still provide valuable insight into Jesus' life and ministry in the Galilee. For that reason, it is certainly worth probing deeper into this story.

The four Gospel accounts parallel each other rather frequently, which isn't surprising considering the fact that all four writers were trying to tell the same story, just in different ways. It is often the case that facts or stories in one Gospel don't appear in the other three, but the opposite can also be true. Such is the case with one story that Matthew, Mark, and John all record, but Luke omits for some reason.

That story is the account of Jesus bodily walking across the surface of the Sea of Galilee. This is probably one of the most popular stories about Jesus in the Gospels. Characteristically, the Gospel of John has some slightly different details than either Matthew or Mark, but the gist of the story remains the same. Matthew's account is the fullest, and it is that version of the story that we will use here.

The night wore on while Jesus prayed on the mountainside. Just before dawn he saw the disciples' boat still struggling to make it across the lake, and he decided to join them for the remainder of their journey. When he got down to the lakeshore, he didn't get into a boat (and not because he was missing the four other crewmen necessary) but rather continued walking, right across the rolling swells.

When he came near the disciples in their boat, they were understandably spooked. They had no idea that Jesus was going to walk across the lake to them, and were equally clueless that walking on water was possible, even for him! Once he identified himself to his followers, however, Peter enthusiastically climbed out of the boat and started walking toward Jesus. He had great faith because it worked at first, but he obviously believed more in the laws of nature than in Jesus at the time. He sank into the Sea of Galilee, and Jesus had to pull him out and bring him to the boat.[4]

This is an incredible story, wonderfully illustrative of the need for faith in Christ. But what does this story from Matthew have to do with the boat in the Yigal Allon Museum? Sure, it's about a boat sailing in the Sea of Galilee, and from the first century A.D. as well. But why this story? There are other stories in the Bible about Jesus in boats on this particular lake.

The answer comes at the end. Matthew slides in a sentence immediately following the story of Jesus walking on water that would probably not catch most people's attention. Chapter 14 Verse 34 states simply, "And when they had crossed over, they came to land at Gennesaret." Of course, the boat that Jesus and his disciples were in had to put in somewhere, so why not Gennesaret? Unless we dig a little deeper, this location doesn't seem important at all.

John's Gospel does say that the place the boat was going to was Capernaum. That's different than what either Matthew or Mark says (both say Gennesaret), but it is still in the same vicinity. Perhaps John indicated Capernaum because it was the closest city that his audience would have recognized. Regardless, Gennesaret on first-century maps of the Galilee is slightly south and west of Capernaum, and a bit northeast of Magdala.

Now compare that map with a modern-day map of the same area. Gennesaret is no longer there, but Ginosar will show up in its place. That's because the two places, Gennesaret and Ginosar, are one and the same.

Gennesaret shows up in only three places in the entire Bible, and the story of Jesus walking on water makes up two of those references, in Matthew and Mark. The third is Luke 5:1, where the Sea of Galilee is referred to as the lake of Gennesaret when Jesus is calling his first disciples. Gennesaret isn't one of the more popular destinations in the Bible, and would certainly be omitted from all Bible maps if not for its brief mention in connection with the "walking on water" story.

Why did Matthew and Mark decide to include the name Gennesaret in their accounts? They could easily have done as John did, naming the nearest big city, a destination that would certainly be more easily recognized by their audiences. The fact that both of these writers mentioned Gennesaret by name means that God wanted it there. Since it didn't seem to be a place of much importance at the time, there must have been another reason why Gennesaret made the scriptural cut.

Perhaps Gennesaret found its way into the Bible because it would be a place of importance at some point in the future. If there were some connection between biblical Gennesaret and modern Ginosar, it would be important to be able to link them together, and the three accounts of Jesus walking on water in Matthew, Mark, and John do just that.

Now, about 2,000 years after the Evangelists penned their narratives, having had them give us the name Gennesaret has proved helpful indeed. Ginosar, its modern counterpart, has become a noteworthy place on the shore of the Sea of Galilee, and all because of a boat. Two fishermen discovered an ancient boat that has been dated to the time of Christ, the only boat of its kind ever to survive. They found it in Ginosar, the same place that was made known nearly two millennia before all because a boat carrying Jesus landed there.

It is entirely possible that the whole thing—a boat pulling into Gennesaret and a boat being pulled out of Ginosar close to 2,000 years later—is simply a coincidence. However, there is more to the story than the few verses allotted to it in the Bible.

The discovery, excavation, and conservation of the boat all seemed providentially guided. No one except the Lufan brothers believed the boat could be saved intact, and seemingly insurmountable obstacles continually threatened the whole process. Yet somehow, despite all of the problems that arose, the boat survived!

What made this boat so special? Why was this the one fishing vessel out of thousands to survive, against all the odds? What protected it until just the right moment that it could be saved?

God did. Everything surrounding the excavation happened just too perfectly, too miraculously to believe that it was all coincidence. Why this particular boat?

Once again, let's return to the story of Jesus walking on water. If ever a boat would survive for nearly 2,000 years in hostile conditions, it seems likely that the boat in question would have been impacted in some miraculous way. There were three events recorded in the Gospels when Jesus performed a miracle at sea. One is the miraculous catch recorded in Luke Chapter 5, immediately following the reference to the lake of Gennesaret. This incident may have happened in the vicinity of Gennesaret, but even so, Luke does not report where the boat came back to land.

The second such event recorded in the Gospels is the famous

calming of the storm. In this episode, Gennesaret is not mentioned; rather, the boat is on its way to "the country of the Gerasenes"[5] across the lake, likely a pagan city because of the abundance of pigs. That leaves one more miraculous story, when Jesus walked on water.

That boat put in at Gennesaret, and that could be the very same vessel that Moishele and Yuvi discovered back in January of 1986.

The coincidence is remarkable, even to the point that it starts to look less and less like a coincidence when you really look into it. While it cannot be proven that the two crafts are the same one, low odds don't mean that it's impossible, though. Having a slim chance might deter a number of people, but it definitely makes things a lot more interesting. One thing is for sure: When the odds are against something, the payoff is going to be big.

———

Sometimes a miracle is simply too fantastic to believe, even when it happens under someone's nose. But not all the time. There is almost always someone who can see and accept the truth for what it is. All it takes is an open heart and a willingness to learn.

Out of everyone who worked on the boat beginning in 1986, Yuvi was the most open for change. He was born and raised in a kibbutz, which if you remember is a secular establishment. When Yuvi was young he asked his father about God, and the answer he got was, "There is no God!" That was all he needed to hear.

Religious Israelis used to visit the kibbutz, and as Yuvi got older he and his friends would challenge them on the existence of God. They weren't afraid to get into heated arguments, and once the visitors were gone Yuvi always felt that he was right. None of their arguments were able to sway his conviction.

Something happened one day that would rattle Yuvi's intellectual and spiritual rigidity, however.

One year on Yom Kippur, shortly after he was married, Yuvi was in a synagogue with many other young Israelis. He was the only non-religious person there, though. All of the other people were singing Jewish songs to celebrate the holiday, but Yuvi did not sing along. As a secular Jew, he did not know the songs, and as the people around him sang he felt nothing. Everyone else was happy and celebrating, but Yuvi did not have anything to celebrate for. As he stood there with everyone around him rejoicing and praising God, he fainted and fell to the floor completely unconscious.

Some of the people in the synagogue finally woke him by splashing water on him. Understandably, Yuvi was shaken. He couldn't think of any explanation for why he had suddenly fainted. He had been feeling fine—the fainting spell had caught him completely unawares. The only reason Yuvi could come up with for his fainting spell was that he had stayed in the synagogue with the believers, while he himself refused to believe in God. He guessed that he fainted because God was upset with his outlook on religion and thought that he should not have been in the synagogue at that time.

Not too long after the fainting episode, Yuvi and his wife moved to Jerusalem for a year. While there, he made contact with a friend who was a rabbi and told him what had happened in the synagogue on Yom Kippur. What the rabbi told him was completely unexpected.

Upon hearing Yuvi's story, the man of faith had only one thought as to what had happened. He told the kibbutznik fisherman that he was a "tzadik", which means "a righteous person" in Hebrew. Yuvi was sure the rabbi was mistaken—in Judaism, tzadik are the most elevated people, very in tune with God and totally focused on Him. Yuvi knew enough about Judaism to be sure that his friend was wrong.

The rabbi was adamant, though. Despite Yuvi's denials, his friend maintained that he was a tzadik. He said that the fact that Yuvi did not believe it did not have any influence on the situation. Compared with the will of God, he was nothing, and if he was chosen for a higher calling, that was the end of the story. He insisted that Yuvi, still a non-believer at that point, would become very close to God in the future.

That was ten years before the two brothers discovered the boat.

Once they found the boat, everything started to fall into place in Yuvi's mind. He realized what his rabbi friend had been talking about—he was chosen to find the boat. In so doing, he was fulfilling God's plan for the ancient craft to be revealed once more to the world, and it was his duty, his calling to make sure it survived.

As a child, Yuvi often visited the holy sites in the vicinity of Ginosar. He liked to go to the Church of the Loaves and Fishes, the presumed location of the feeding of the five thousand, and think about who had been there before. For some reason, even though he was not a Christian, Yuvi was drawn to the sites commonly identified with the beginnings of Christian faith.

The discovery of the boat brought everything together for him. His youthful appreciation of the Christian holy sites and the rabbi's assertion of his righteous and spiritual nature all started to make sense. Especially as Yuvi witnessed the excavation of the boat and all of the miracles that happened to keep it alive, he realized that God had his hand in the process. Not only that, he was acutely aware of the fact that he was involved in part of God's plan. To paraphrase Yuvi's words, "none of these things happened without a purpose."

The recognition that God was guiding both the excavation and the people working on the boat was too much for him to ignore. No longer was the idea of God an impersonal, distant thought. For Yuvi, God was right there in the mud, working to save the boat and using the volunteers as tools to reach that goal.

In his mind, there wasn't any doubt as to why God would want this boat to be rescued. It had important spiritual significance, and it was an artifact that could be used to bring people closer to God. After all, it had done so for him—why not for others as well? Yuvi remembered the stories he had heard at times over the years, stories about Jesus walking on water and calming the sea, particularly the story of how Jesus had fed five thousand men with five fish and two loaves of bread. As he remembered each story, he knew in his heart that they were all true.

———

Is it too far-fetched for Yuvi to believe that the boat had survived because Jesus had used it in his ministry in the Galilee? He doesn't think so.

Yuvi's story is incredible: He went from being an atheist in a Jewish country to someone who believes that Jesus is more than a name out of the history books. This boat brought Jesus' world to life for Yuvi, a man who spent all his days where Jesus had walked. What he and his brother found made the whole world of the Bible real for him—he felt connected with the fishermen of old, with the Disciples, and with Jesus.

That's what this boat can do for people. It isn't something that will guarantee a closer walk with Jesus, more discipline in devotions or an increased desire to follow God's will. Touching the boat isn't like the Midas touch. It won't heal sicknesses, and it won't spawn untold wealth. What it can do, however, is helpful for living a life after Jesus' model.

This boat is a touch point to Jesus' ministry on Earth. Much as excavations in Jerusalem allow visitors to see the level of the streets as they were when Christ healed sick people and walked the Via Dolorosa, this ancient fishing vessel shows anyone who wants to see what means Jesus had available to him. Jesus may or may not have used this particular boat—that may never be conclusively proven either way. However, it is an example of what our Lord slept in while a sharkia raged on the lake, and it is the same kind of boat that almost sank because of a miraculous catch of fish.

This fantastic discovery allows everyone who wishes to better relate to the people that Jesus knew and lived with. As it did for Yuvi Lufan, this boat can bring the Bible to life in a more vivid and visible way than it was before. Seeing a boat like this makes it easier to see the disciples almost crippled by fear because of a powerful storm. But like the ancient storm that put the fear of God into those twelve men, time has swept away any clues that would provide a concrete answer to the biggest question raised by this boat: Was this Jesus' boat?

The circumstances around this boat provide no proof to answer that question. Such proof relies totally on personal belief, based in turn upon faith. But doesn't that sound familiar?

Epilogue:

𝄞

SEEING IS BELIEVING

I must admit, when I first heard about this, I was pretty skeptical. I was in Israel for the first time traveling with my family, and we were told that we needed to go to the Yigal Allon Museum to check the boat out. As a Christian, there were other sites around the Sea of Galilee I felt my time would be better spent at, but regardless of that I had to see the boat.

I had heard about the boat a little bit: that it had been excavated under extraordinary circumstances and that it had been dated to around the time of Christ's earthly ministry. I knew that some people drew parallels to Jesus because of the boat's age, but I thought that was pretty far-fetched. After all, there must have been dozens, if not hundreds of boats in use at that time, and there was no way to prove a connection to Jesus conclusively, one way or the other.

When we arrived at the museum, we went straight back to see the exhibit with the boat. The exhibit room is laid out so that you watch a short movie about the excavation before you walk up to the boat, so I had an opportunity to learn a bit more before I saw it for the first time. I was blown away by what I heard and saw in the movie. The people were so genuine, and their love for this boat was so apparent. There must be something special about it after all.

Once the movie was over, I walked over to have a look at the boat. There wasn't as much of it left as I had expected, just a worn-down hull that had clearly seen better days. As I looked at it, a projector displayed on the wall behind the boat the mosaic from

With the Migdal mosaic projected behind it, the boat sits on display in the Yigal Allon Museum

Migdal, slowly turning into a reproduction of what the hull would have looked like whole.

I had to hold back my tears.

When the depiction was complete, a boat just like the one Jesus would have used was projected just behind the artifact I was staring at. For the first time, I believed that what rested directly in front of me could have been one of the boats used by my Savior in the Gospels, and I was overwhelmed.

Over the course of my time writing this book, I have come to learn even more about this boat. By itself, it has an incredible story—countless times while writing I found myself wishing I had been old enough during the excavation to be there myself. Even so, this boat has become a treasure for me. I know that I cannot know for certain who used this boat, but it is enough for me to be able to think who may have used it. This boat brings me back to the first century A.D. on the Sea of Galilee in a new, tangible way.

People can see this boat and understand the terror the disciples felt before Christ woke up and calmed the storming seas. It allows everyone to better grasp the world the disciples were called out of, as well as the world they were sent back into. It lets us see in more detail how totally dependent Galileans in the first century were on the lake, and how much of a sacrifice it was for the first disciples to abandon their livelihoods and their families to follow Jesus.

This boat's biggest contribution to Christianity is the connection it provides for Christians today with their counterparts from Bible times. It brings their world to life in a way that text alone cannot.

But there is more to the story of this boat than ancient wood. The archaeologists and the people at Ginosar are what brought the boat to its place in the museum. God gave them the strength and the means, and they used what they were given and made sure the boat, despite the challenges they were faced with, would survive. Best of all, it had a profound impact on their lives as well.

Ginosar continues to rally around the boat, and it is significant that it remains on exhibit there. The members of the kibbutz may often be seen in the museum, and it isn't uncommon to run into one of the Lufan brothers by the boat. They are incredible men, and if you visit the boat, try to meet one of them. God has already used this amazing vessel to change Yuvi's life—it is waiting to impact others as well.

There will always be skeptics about this story. Everything about it seems too good to be true. Even I was doubtful about the boat's importance before I had seen it. Putting all that aside, though, one thing is for sure: This is a truly special boat, and its story is awe-inspiring. No matter what anyone says, it is one of the biggest miracles outside of the Bible.

Important Names

Yuvi and Moishele Lufan—Kibbutznik brothers who discovered the boat
Yantshe Lufan—The brothers' father
Nitza Kaplan—Manager of the Yigal Allon Museum
Mendel Nun—Local kibbutznik expert on the Sea of Galilee
Avner Raban—Archaeologist who thought the boat was modern
Kurt Raveh—Lead archaeologist
Shelley Wachsmann—Lead archaeologist
Orna Cohen—Ship's conservator
Richard Steffy—Renowned ship reconstructor
Avi Eitan—Director of the Department of Antiquities
Thomas Pickering—U.S. Ambassador to Israel
Arye Nehemkin—Israeli Minister of Agriculture
Yitzhak Navon—Israeli Minister of Education
Zvi Ortenberg—Director of the Kinneret Authority

Notes

3. Page 98 Daily Life in the Time of Jesus pg. 273

CHAPTER 6: BUILD ME A BOAT

1. Page 103 Adan-Bayewitz, David pg. 89

2. Page 104 Adan-Bayewitz, David pg. 89, 92

3. Page 105 Adan-Bayewitz, David pg. 93

4. Page 106 Wachsmann pg. 181

5. Page 107 Sussman, Varda pg. 97–98

6. Page 109 Steffy, Richard. pg. 37

7. Page 110 Steffy, Richard pg. 37

8. Page 112 Steffy, Richard pg. 37

9. Page 115 Wachsmann pg. 301

10. Page 116 Wachsmann pg. 304

11. Page 118 Wachsmann pg. 306

CHAPTER 7: A BATH FOR A BOAT

1. Page 126 Wachsmann pg. 267

2. Page 129 Wachsmann pg. 271

3. Page 131 Wachsmann pg. 273

4. Page 132 Wachsmann pg. 283

5. Page 134 Wachsmann pg. 285

6. Page 136 Wachsmann pg. 291

7. Page 138 Wachsmann pg. 294

8. Page 141 Wachsmann pg. 296–297

Trusting God In Every Situation

1. Page 149 Luke 5: 4–9

CHAPTER 9: MIRACLES, MIRACLES, MIRACLES!

1. Page 168 Wachsmann pg. 85

2. Page 173 Wachsmann pg. 33

NOTES

Putting Aside All Fear

1. Page 177 Mark 4: 37–41

CHAPTER 10: MAKING WAVES

1. Page 183 Wachsmann pg. 315
2. Page 183 Mark 1:16–18
3. Page 184 Mark 1:20
4. Page 185 Matthew 14:22–33
5. Page 188 Mark 5:1

BIBLIOGRAPHY

Wachsmann, Shelley. The Sea of Galilee Boat: An Extraordinary 2000-Year-Old Discovery. New York: Plenum Press, 1995.

All biblical quotations are taken from the following: The Holy Bible: English Standard Version. Wheaton, Illinois: Good News Publishers, 2007.

Daniel-Rops, Henri. Daily Life In The Time Of Jesus. Trans. Patrick O'Brian. New York: Hawthorn Books, 1962.

Lohse, Eduard. The New Testament Environment. Trans. John E. Steely. Nashville: Abingdon, 1976.

Adan-Bayewitz, David. "The Excavations of an Ancient Boat in the Sea of Galilee (Lake Sea of Galilee)."Atiqot English Series Volume XIX (1990).

Sussman, Varda. "The Excavations of an Ancient Boat in the Sea of Galilee (Lake Sea of Galilee)."Atiqot English Series Volume XIX (1990).

Steffy, Richard. "The Excavations of an Ancient Boat in the Sea of Galilee (Lake Sea of Galilee)."Atiqot English Series Volume XIX (1990).

PHOTOGRAPH CREDITS

All images courtesy of the IAA (Israeli Antiquities Authority), formerly known as the Israeli Department of Antiquities.